MORNING

CATHY PETERS

This 20-year-long passion project was the result of a compilation of personal notes and journal entries, along with our children's unedited journals, from 1999–2000 when our family sailed away for a one-year adventure.

I hope you will enjoy traveling vicariously with our family as we sought to do something unique and memorable together.

This book is dedicated to our children—Joshua, Joanna, and Lydia—who were the primary reason for our trip; to my fearless and detail-oriented husband Allan who made it happen; to all the cruisers who helped and inspired us along the way; and to the maritime professionals who keep our seas safe and protected.

—Cathy Peters

MORNING

Twenty years from now you will be more disappointed by the things that you didn't do than by the ones you did do. So throw off the bow-lines. Sail away from the safe harbour. Catch the trade winds in your sails.
Explore. Dream. Discover.

—*Mark Twain*

CHAPTER 1

Humpbacks

Our first contact with humpback whales occurred north of San Francisco. It was an unexpected encounter on an "extreme weather" sailing day down the U.S. west coast.

We moored for the night in the Fort Bragg Marine Basin. We left the small marina by 05:30 and our destination was south to Bodega Bay with its large secure marina. We thought we could easily transit during daylight hours.

It was a clear day to sail. This was a relief to us because Northern Californian coastline conditions are typically foggy and windy.

We motored *Morning*, our 44-foot Nordic sailboat, for a few hours until the wind piped up. It was 15 knots, then crept up to the 20 knot range, and settled back down to 15 knots.[1]

Allan had to work very hard on sailing the boat downwind, bringing sails in and out. He finally set up the spinnaker wing-on-wing. *Morning* looked like a giant bird wallowing in the building waves. We rolled around a lot, but

---

[1]Wind at 15 knots (28 km/hr) can be comfortable with all the sails up. I call it "dream sailing." I am not very happy when the wind speed reaches 25 knots (46 km/hr). The sails need to be made quite small (reefed) and in the open ocean, the seas will be very large. With 34 knots (63 km/hr) or gale force, the seas get huge, and sailing becomes difficult for a small crew. It's time to be safely anchored somewhere.

as we turned the corner at Point Arena we were running with the swell and it became a smooth, comfortable sail.

The wind increased suddenly. At 25 knots, it's time to reduce the sails. The waves became steep and built up to over eight feet high at five seconds apart. Now it was going to be a real challenge to reef the sails.

Allan swung the boat at an angle in waves and wind so that *Morning* stayed in a reasonably stationary position. We were able to safely reef the main and gyb sail. This manoeuver demanded full attention, strength, and concentration. We should have pulled the sails in much sooner before the wind built up and the waves got so large. We were sailing in rapidly deteriorating sea conditions. My heart was pounding and I struggled to stay focused. This was the most challenging sailing we had ever done.

With three children on board I could have panicked, but I forced my fear down. I had to be fully functioning and alert in order to assist Allan with managing the boat.

As Allan was tugging on one of the lines he screamed, "Something black, dead ahead!" In spectacular simultaneous motion two enormous black humpback whales breached directly in front of our boat. They fell on to their backs with a gigantic splash. Unexpectedly, one of the whales came alongside our rapidly moving boat. We were barrelling down the face of the wave at record speed with this huge whale right beside us. Meanwhile, Allan was doing his best to keep the boat under control.

Our children were so excited that they were hanging over the side of our boat to get as close as they could to the humpback whale. Normally the children would have been harnessed and tethered to the boat so they wouldn't slip overboard, but everything was happening so fast.

We could see one whale eye and we were close enough to smell the whale's breath. I was horrified. I imagined that in one quick flick the gargantuan tail would smash our boat to bits.

Joshua, Joanna, and Lydia were ecstatic—to be so close to a large humpback whale was exhilarating. Who at home would believe this? No aquarium experience was even close.

Abruptly, with a big snort and deep breath, the mammoth creature slipped away under the water and disappeared.

We were stunned, hardly able to believe what we had seen. My heart was pounding, concerned that the children were still not tethered to the boat. Would the whale resurface? We scanned the horizon looking for signs of the great humpbacks.

I scooted the children down below while Allan and I got back to concentrate on sailing our erratically surfing sailboat.

Up and down monstrous seas we raced up to eleven knots—faster than the speed at which the boat was designed to sail.

We barely caught our breath when a pod of 10 porpoises arrived and surrounded our boat. They swam alongside us for a half an hour as *Morning* wildly careened down the waves.

To have these frolicking visitors accompany us was wonderful. It felt like the ocean was offering up her inhabitants so that our little family would not be so overwhelmed by a large, threatening, dark ocean.

Surprisingly I found it a great comfort to know that we were not alone on that tumultuous churning grey sea.

We left quite early in the morning because it was a full day of travel. The trip started with rolly waters and no wind. Near breakfast time the wind kicked up to 15 knots. We pulled out all our sails. We looked at the wind indicator again and it was 25 knots!! We reefed the sails. The wind got stronger we reefed some more. Soon the wind got up to 30 knots. Dad was reefing the main sail and suddenly shouted. Now, our dad is not a shouter so we thought the rigging was falling down or something worse. We looked out to sea and suddenly we saw it too. It was a big black thing leaping out of the water. Dad had thought at first it was a rock or ship but soon we realized it was two humpback whales breaching right out of the water. They passed us by waving their long beautiful flippers at us. Later that day porpoises also came to play in our bow wake to make sure we were okay. Our friends on *Saucy Lady* were sailing behind us and the porpoises and humpbacks gave them a show, too, how fun.

Along the way we have seen over a dozen whales just look at us and leave. We even smelt their breath though it wasn't very nice. Dolphins and porpoises keep us busy too, riding the bow wake. They can go faster than our boat even at our fastest speed. Aren't those whales amazing!!!!!????

There is nothing, absolutely nothing, half so much worth doing as simply messing about in boats.

—Kenneth Grahame, *Wind in the Willows*

CHAPTER 2

Beginnings

Five years earlier we bought our first sailboat. It was a small boat, 23 feet in length. Allan "got a deal" one weekend from an acquaintance we knew on Bowen Island. He paid $2,500 for the boat. We named her *Swallow*. Apparently, in nautical tradition all boats are considered female.

Allan was thrilled with this new acquisition, because it gave our family an easy way to get away and have adventures. With years of reading the British children's sailing series *Swallows and Amazons* our family was ready to head out on our own *Swallow*.

Allan got us sailing as often as he could with the goal of planning longer trips.

He planned our first overnight weekend trip away to Brigade Bay on Gambier Island. It was only a few miles from our home on Bowen Island.

I organized the food, sleeping gear, clothing for all variety of weather conditions for each of us, as well as a packing up a compass, and a chart.

We headed off. This was our first family sailing adventure.

It took us three hours to get to Gambier Island. We learned years later that this trip would take half an hour.

The trip to Brigade Bay was long, but uneventful. The children were very excited. Once we anchored in the bay, we took quite a bit of time to get organized for the night. It was a logistical exercise to find a sleeping corner for everyone on board this cramped but cosy 23-foot boat. Allan and I slept in the small open cockpit with a tarp over us in a tent fashion. The children slept inside the boat, and all of our gear was piled up on the small table inside the middle of the boat.

We did not take into account that the Sea-to-Sky Highway was directly opposite the anchorage. We listened to traffic all night; it was a sleepless night.

In the morning we woke up to six inches of icy cold ocean water on the floor of the boat. I have never experienced anything so unpleasant. Our children were undaunted. It was our first overnight on a boat. "Dad, could we do more of this, please?" they pleaded.

After a summer of sailing *Swallow*, Allan realized she wasn't a **real** sailboat. It seemed to take us forever to cover any distance at all. With all the sails up *Swallow* hardly moved. With a strong current against us we did not move in a forward direction. Allan was frustrated and renamed her "The Slug."

Yet Allan had a dream. *Cruising World* magazine described a sailing dreamland that was beyond our limited Howe Sound waters. Allan wanted to experience sailing dreamland.

We have a friend who was a boat broker. Without telling me, Allan was talking with this man about boats.

One day Allan came home and announced that we had bought a boat for $70,000 (in 1995 dollars).

He had not discussed this with me. I was shocked at this huge investment.

"But, honey, we HAVE a boat!" I replied naively and with irritation in my voice. I could not believe he went ahead and made such a large purchase with no discussion.

"Cathy, I've bought our family a great boat. One that can actually go places... you know... wilderness places, and faraway places, like when you circumnavigate," Allan ended triumphantly.

I didn't get it.

"How much bigger, Allan? How big is this boat?" By this point I was impatient and pressing.

"Cathy, this is a *sail* boat; a 39-foot C&C. It raced in the Vic-Maui race. She can really move. She'll be perfect for our family. And we can go away for weeks at a time."

I was stunned. To go from 23-foot *Swallow*, that could hardly move forward in a good wind, to a Vic-Maui racing machine seemed like a huge leap.

I gulped. This was the first step towards "The Dream."

So *Swallow* was sold. And *Seraphim* became our new family member. Allan loved our new boat. And he bought dinghies—for the children, of course—that he named *Seraph* and *Sera*.

I started to realize Allan wanted to do more with his life than just work all the time. He wanted to give something significant to our children. He wanted them to know the joy of sailing that he had experienced when he went to summer sailing camp at 12 years of age. Allan wanted our children to experience life; full life on the edge. I call it "the living in the moment" kind of life. He wanted our children, while they were still young, to experience the kind of life that requires focus, discipline, dedication, challenge, and hard work; real life living that you work hard at for those experiences that you never forget.

It wasn't long before Allan had a subscription to *Pacific Yachting Magazine* and *Cruising World Magazine*. He signed up with the local Bluewater Cruising Association. Allan attended all the meetings in Vancouver. He took every course offered including diesel mechanics, navigation, and wilderness medicine.

Allan was committed to a dream. He wanted his family to sail and to sail away to **somewhere**. I needed to know exactly what he was thinking. What did he have in mind?

I did not know how to sail and had only been on a small sailboat a couple of times in my life. I had not particularly enjoyed the experience. As a matter of fact, I did not like it at all. I had memories of being cold and wet and not being able to get to the destination planned on. I knew that you cannot sail in a straight line to anything. Zig-zagging to a destination seemed pointless in my mind.

Sailing is dependent on the wind. And the wind is unpredictable if there is any wind at all. There is either no wind or too much wind. I never understood people who were passionate about sailing. And I was discovering that I was married to a man who thought he loved sailing. Maybe he was in love with the idea of sailing to those exotic places that were featured on the colourful yachting magazine covers.

Admittedly, our experience with *Swallow* and *Seraphim* proved that our children loved sailing. They loved the adventure, the fun of being together, all cozy, doing outdoor adventures and having amazing outings. It gave them a strong sense of freedom and adventure they had never experienced before. They were taking responsibility with boat chores, their journal writing, living together in tight quarters, and getting along with each other. The skills we were learning by sailing were changing our family into a cooperative team unit. Everyone had to pitch in and work together. They got really excited about it all. Reading adventure books out loud to them for years beforehand had probably contributed to this appetite for the "real adventure." Now they were ready to do it.

I went along with the plan.

If we were going to sail as a family I made the decision that at least I would make sure our children knew how to sail. I signed them up for every sailing course I could find. I also signed them up for every level of swimming lesson. I had to know they would be safe and comfortable on the water. Lydia, our youngest, was not that happy with the prospect of sailing or swimming lessons, but she never complained to me. She did her part and went along with her brother and sister.

I took the Basic Power Squadron Course offered locally. A good friend of ours also attended the course. Chris had grown up sailing in the Atlantic Ocean off of Great Britain. He was most encouraging and said, "Yes, Cathy, you will be able to sail across Georgia Strait. Your boat can do it, so, you can too."

I wasn't sure what Chris meant. Georgia Strait is that large expanse of water (20 miles across) between Vancouver Island and the BC mainland, which ferries cross. In my mind this was not a stretch of water that a small sailboat should be crossing—especially with young children on board.

I passed the Power Squadron course with 100 per cent. At least I knew the theory of basic boating, safety and navigation.

Meanwhile, Allan was planning our next boating adventure; two months of summer sailing as far as we could go in our local waters. Allan bought all the charts for the Gulf Islands, San Juan Islands, Desolation Sound, Princess Louisa Inlet, and even further north.

Allan was getting very serious about this.

He outfitted the boat so it worked well and he set it up so that it would be comfortable for living on board. As an architect, Allan is a "detail" man. He knows how to think about and deal with all the smallest details. He is also handy and can fix anything. This was a comfort to me. At least I knew we had a boat that would work and that Allan could fix.

Once school was out at the end of June it took a couple of weeks to get the boat loaded up and well provisioned before we set off for two months of sailing by mid-July.

I had no idea what the two months ahead would be or could be like living on a sailboat. I had never grown up on boats. This was the most unfamiliar experience I had ever had. How would I manage? How would the family manage? How would the children do away from home routines? What would happen if I hated it? I had a lot of questions and concerns. It was all overwhelming.

Allan meticulously organized everything and before I knew it we were sailing across Georgia Strait to Vancouver Island. With the ferries. The boat sailed beautifully because she was designed to sail really well. In fact, we easily sailed past most boats wherever we went. *Seraphim* was like a flying machine. Her hull sliced effortlessly through the water and we were able to cover a lot of distance in no time. It was exhilarating.

We had an unbelievably magical summer with our family. We discovered every corner of Desolation Sound, Princess Louisa Inlet, the Gulf Islands, and some of the San Juan Islands. We kept our children out of school in September for three weeks. What we learned and gained during that two months away was immeasurable.

To young men contemplating a voyage I would say go.

—*Joshua Slocum*

CHAPTER 3

Morning

After our magical summer on Seraphim, Allan was doing more thinking. "I don't think *Seraphim* is the right boat for us, Cathy," Allan mused.

"Allan, you are kidding. What are you thinking? We had a perfect summer on Seraphim. She is a wonderful boat for us."

"Well, we can't go offshore with her. There is not enough deck space for the dinghies and there's not enough room on her for us all to be comfortable on a long term voyage."

"Allan, how long term are you thinking? Where do you hope to go?"

"I'd like to have a boat that could sail around the world if we wanted to. But at the very least, that it would be comfortable going offshore."

So, there it was. He said it: Offshore Sailing.

That was the dream and his plan.

I knew Allan was feeling dissatisfied with the school system and our children's peer groups. I knew he wanted our children to understand that there is a much bigger world to experience and explore.

I did not take time to process all of this because I couldn't process it. It was too much and too fast for me to figure out. I was not a sailor but I wanted to support Allan. I instinctively felt that a year away with our children on a sailboat would be a remarkable once-in-a lifetime experience. Allan is the sailor and could run the boat. I had full confidence that somehow we could do it. I simply felt it was the right thing to do for our family.

I was tentative, but agreed with The Dream.

We started to make specific plans. The age of our children would be the determining factor.

"Cathy, we can't leave it too late. We have to do it ideally before they reach the teen years. I want our children to have a strong foundation so they are equipped for the teen years and beyond."

It made sense what Allan was proposing. I did understand and had to agree with him.

The problem was we needed a different boat. This meant selling *Seraphim* and looking for a more suitable boat. We needed something that was larger and beamier (wider). And it was probably going to be a lot more expensive.

Allan pored over boat journals. He spent hours researching and looking for the right boat. He talked to people he knew who boated. He talked to cruisers he met at Blue Water Cruising Association who had sailed offshore. He asked for advice from everyone he could think of.

When he didn't expect it he found *Morning* described in a boat journal. It was the perfect boat for what he wanted us to do.

Morning is a 44-foot Nordic sloop designed by distinguished naval architect Robert Perry. The Nordic is a proven design for an offshore sailing vessel.

Morning was moored in Bellingham just south of Vancouver. A retired neurosurgeon owned the boat and had sailed single-handed around Cape Horn from Hawaii to the Caribbean. There was a lot of distance under her keel. She was an ideal vessel for offshore sailing. The owner now had health issues and was anxious to sell her.

Allan bought *Morning* and with our boat broker friend, his son, and our daughter Joanna, they sailed *Morning* back to Bowen Island via the Gulf Islands. It took a couple of days to get to Bowen Island with a very successful comfortable Georgia Strait crossing.

Allan was absolutely delighted with her. *Morning* was a true offshore sailboat. She was a **real** sailboat; spacious, comfortable, and stable. *Morning* could handle any sea and weather conditions safely. Allan had found the dream boat for our family.

But, *Morning* needed a lot of work done. She was a tired and well-worn boat. Although *Morning* was sound, she needed a major refit and became a project for Allan for the next three years. Allan replaced everything; wiring, plumbing, rigging, and sails. To be self-sufficient Allan added a watermaker, solar panels, wind generator, autopilot, and a single sideband radio. Allan bought all the emergency gear he could think of. Then he thought of additional details that would make a lengthy trip comfortable: fans, screens, plenty of storage area, new cook top, refrigeration system, secure hatches to prevent leakage, and furling sails. He made sure we had three dinghies; one for each child. This would give each child the freedom to leave our boat when we anchored and they could feel independent. Allan collected extra parts for everything. He even learnt how to take the engine transmission out to have it rebuilt at a specialist shop.

Allan worked hard in our design and construction business. He wanted to have the financial resources to take a long trip away. His thought was to aim to leave by June 1999. Joshua would be finished Grade 7 and elementary school, Joanna would be finished Grade 5, and Lydia would be finished Grade 3. He thought these were perfect ages for our children to go on an offshore trip.

Allan calculated that if we rented out our house for the time we were away, it would help to cover our costs of travel, especially if we stayed away from marinas. By this time he had read a lot of books about how to do this and he was convinced it was viable.

One question troubled me: How long would we go for?

I settled it with Allan that I would take each section of travel and evaluate it at the time. So, for example, we would begin with a circumnavigation of Vancouver Island for the summer. Then we would evaluate whether it was prudent to continue our travels south. The next stretch would be the west coast of the U.S. to San Diego. We would then evaluate at San Diego. The next significant stretch would be Mexico. At the one year point we could evaluate the whole experience and decide if we wanted to make the 3 week open ocean crossing to the South Pacific via the Marqueses Islands or return home.

Our trip began.

LYDIA'S JOURNAL

I will tell my readers what I think about our trip. I think it is a good experience for young people and I think that families should be doing things together.

Joshua said to me that we were the Swiss Family Robinson or the Swiss Family Peters for some weird reason (well, just for a joke he thought it was pretty funny).

BRITISH COLUMBIA, CANADA

When a man comes to like a sea life,
he is not fit to live on land.

—*Samuel Johnson*

CHAPTER 4

Black and White

Any trip will begin with a list of things that need to get done. The list began a year before our departure. While Allan managed to prepare the boat he also finished projects to make our house ready to rent. He took the advanced boating courses, got his HAM radio license, wrapped up his business, packed up his office, moved our furniture out of our house, pumped out our septic tank, simplified our finances, and packed up the boat. We wrote our wills.

I still had routines to maintain while organizing sailing lessons, swimming lessons, ongoing piano practising, school projects, choir practices and performances, and school sports with constant chauffeuring. There were birthday parties, and we had visitors to entertain.

I needed to organize school correspondence courses and collect a supply of books to have on board for our children to read.

We managed to get our shots for prevention of tropical diseases, correspondence organized, house, car, and travel insurance set up, a Master Book organized for ourselves and for my mom (our executor), and a detailed House Book written for our house renters explaining how our home worked. I booked haircuts, dental, and orthodontics appointments. We washed and packed all of our clothes. Our house furnishings were boxed and labeled in order to store in our garage. We serviced our cars and put up them up on blocks, also in the garage. We figured out what to take with us for the year. We said our goodbyes.

We rented our house within a few days of our ad being placed in the local paper. The renters were a young couple from Ontario. We left our home and belongings in good hands. We appreciated all the little thank yous and helps from people in our community. We had been quiet about our plans until the last few months leading up to our departure. The logistics of planning and preparing a trip like this with children can be daunting. But we managed it, slowly ticking off each item on our long to-do list.

Allan got five van loads packed on to our boat. He patiently wedged things into every conceivable nook and cranny. We used a vast assortment of Rubbermaid containers. Allan drew a detailed map to show where everything on the boat was stowed. Stowing items conveniently was a giant complicated exercise that resembled playing three-dimensional chess.

JOANNA'S JOURNAL

Today was just a regular day, but for me it was exciting because we are leaving on Monday or Tuesday. We got loaded up with another load from the house to the boat. And… guess what? Our boat has sunk six inches with all the storage! Pretty exciting. We still have all our clothes and bedding to be loaded on.

JOSHUA'S JOURNAL

Last preparation days before leaving: I really like working with Dad on our boat and I know he needs my help and company.

But what freedom! To think that all the energy put into living, running a business, serving clients, building houses, running a home, providing for the children, organizing lessons, planning get-togethers, maintaining traditions, keeping up with myriad people, friends and family… all that energy was now focused into managing our boat, and being a family, with no schedule. Just going with the weather while trusting God to lead, protect, and direct us. From our limited life experience it was a remarkable feat to attempt and over time proved to be providential.

On June 14, 1999 we untied the lines and left the dock from Snug Cove Marina, Bowen Island. We had a quiet calm crossing of Georgia Strait.

JOANNA'S JOURNAL

We proceeded to cross the Strait. It was as flat as glass. What a beautiful crossing that was. The sky was like a great grey roof, it was so flat. We are almost there. We will anchor in Degnen Bay for the night. I feel so happy because we are finally off!

We have done a lot of good-byes, hugging and saying "Goodbye, and have a fun time" and things like that that is normal with "Good-byes." Today we're heading North. Three cheers to Port Hardy!

Wow! Guess what? We saw at least 20 to 30 killer whales at Campbell River. They were all around the boat it was awesome! They are so graceful, just so intelligent, so here is what happened: We were on our way to Gowland Harbour we saw a splash ahead. A big one, too! "Whales, Whales" Joshua yells and sure as can be a whole pod of whales—killer whales—come leaping, diving and swimming towards us. We were up so close that we could see them move under the water!

JOSHUA'S JOURNAL

It is going to take us seven hours to reach Cape Mudge, on the southern end of Quadra Island. I'm so, so happy. I'm going to visit my Camp Homewood (childhood summer camp). On the way up we saw penguin-like birds, seal covered rocks and boats of all kinds. Then in Discovery Passage, guess what happened? We happened upon a big pod of killer whales. This was the first time that I'd ever seen them in the wild. They are amazing, graceful creatures.

We motored all the way up to the north tip of Vancouver Island. It was completely calm. We made excellent time travelling a couple hundred miles in a few days. It was fun to pass the "Round Vancouver Island Sailing Race" vessels. They struggled to make any headway since there was hardly a trace of wind.

As we left familiar Georgia Strait and came up to Seymour Narrows, opposite Campbell River, we saw a pod of orcas swimming towards us. Their sleek bodies are a distinctive black and white coloring. They smoothly skimmed and bobbed along the water surface then neatly ducked right underneath our boat. It was as though they were coming to say "hello," and "have a good trip." They were deliberate in swimming directly to us. Then they raced away into the expanse of Georgia Strait. It felt like we were in a dream or time warp when time stops for a while. We were in the wilderness seeing wildlife close up. The children were thrilled. Journal writing became something to look forward to because they always had something exciting to write about.

Johnstone Strait is the next long stretch of water that follows half the length of Vancouver Island. It is notorious for bad weather. It is a tricky stretch because it is narrow. However, we had no problem and easily made the 100-mile run up the Strait. We motored at 12 knots thanks to the current pushing us.

As we got closer to Port Hardy, Allan decided to pull out the sails for the first time. The mainsail got stuck in the furling, which is the mechanical system that neatly wraps the huge mainsail inside a tall slender canister attached to the mast. It was a disaster. How could we sail anywhere when we could not get the huge mainsail in and out of the mast furling?

Just before leaving home one of the last things that Allan had done was to put a U.V. protective coating on all the sails' stitching. It had not cured properly and the mainsail remained sticky. The result was that it became impossible to pull the mainsail in or out of the furling.

Slowly, with a great deal of care and patience, Allan managed to furl the mainsail in. We sat in completely calm water waiting for Allan to tuck in the sail. At the same time a large crowd of 40 to 50 porpoises unexpectedly surfaced around us. With incredible choreography they began leaping, jumping, turning, spinning, flipping, and blowing. They displayed marvelous agility and energy. The porpoises were black, with patches of white and grey. Streamlined forms flowed together in one fluid rhythm. They swam around and around and under our boat. Time seemed to stop for us and our children were enthralled with the show.

Once Allan had the sail in place we motored to Port Hardy directly to the public docks. Upon docking, Joshua spent the next hour winching Allan up the tall mast to pull out the mainsail to unfurl, furl, and refurl until we knew it would work with no trouble. We took a day to reprovision at Port Hardy and get our laundry done before heading towards Cape Scott, the northern point of Vancouver Island.

We had been away for seven days and had seen more wildlife than most people see in a lifetime. For me, so far, this sailing trip was far beyond my wildest dreams.

There was only one problem: we hadn't started sailing yet.

The sea finds out everything you did wrong.

—*Francis Stokes*

CHAPTER 5

Open Ocean

We are in God's Pocket. Just before going around Cape Scott. It is Father's Day on our boat! I gave Dad a card in calligraphy. Dads are so-o-o special and I love mine (as all children should) and a little extra too! This morning we had pancakes. That's a big treat for us!

We left Port Hardy and headed for a tiny protected anchorage called "God's Pocket." It is located at the northern tip of Vancouver Island and the weather was noticeably colder. A front was coming through with winds and rain. It was time to prepare for heading into the open ocean for our first time. Allan got the weather cloths strapped around the cockpit. He practised putting the storm staysail and storm trysail up, installed extra latches and hooks on inside doors, and reorganized more storage cupboards. He prepared a convenient spot for our garbage, attached straps for the kitchen and navigation table, and secured wooden handholds throughout our cabin.

We left at 08:00 heading into Queen Charlotte Sound. We needed to go around Cape Scott to reach our destination: Sea Otter Cove. It is a 58-mile stretch. The forecast was for southwest winds and big ocean swells. It was going to be a wild day on the ocean.

The mainsail furling continued to be sticky going in and out. The diesel fuel stove filled the cabin with smoke. A hose came off in the bathroom, so we had a flood. All of this occurred while the waves and driving wind picked up. This was our "shakedown" cruise (shake-up? break-down? throw-up!).

The children kept doing schoolwork down below while it was really rough outside. Joshua helped to mop up the flood. This triggered upset tummies and the children had to lie down for the next 6-7 hours of the trip. Joshua and Lydia held out, but then threw up at the end of the day. The overly sweet granola bars at lunchtime didn't help.

Many lessons were learned rounding the infamous Cape Scott. Allan did course and plotting work while underway. This should have been done before we left. The children needed to have their secure spot and stay put. We were all moving around too much while sailing. The motion on the open ocean can be violent especially when you are in a small boat. Inside the boat it felt like we were inside a washing machine. Schoolwork cannot be done. The heating stove needs to be off and every loose item stowed away. Furling the sails needs to be carefully done.

At this point I prayed, "God, help us." There was so much to learn. More than anything I wanted this to be a safe and positive family experience. I also needed to be able to help Allan run the boat, day after day.

When we rounded Cape Scott the sun came out and porpoises leapt around the boat. I felt that they were celebrating with us. We had made it around this renowned and dangerous point of land (see Chapter 15).

JOANNA'S JOURNAL

My Mom is triumphant now because we actually went around Cape Scott! "We did it", that's what we all kept saying. Three dolphins came round our boat for a minute. It cheered everybody up.

During storms and in the winter season, this part of the ocean at the northern tip of Vancouver Island has the reputation for the largest waves in the world. While we were careful to wait for reasonable conditions we were not unaware of the challenges of sailing in this area. I was thankful for our seaworthy and sea-proven boat. I was also deeply appreciative of the meticulous preparation by our skipper, Dad.

JOSHUA'S JOURNAL

As soon as we got into Queen Charlotte Sound we were in open ocean and the big ocean swells started. To make a long story short we saw porpoises when rounding Cape Scott, Lydia and I got quite sick and no one felt very good except for our hero, Mom. Sea Otter Cove is beautiful. But there are so many rocks and the beaches, I've never seen the like of them in my entire life.

Sea Otter Cove is a cute, tucked away anchorage with "bomb-proof" mooring buoys for the fishing fleet. But what a tricky place to get in to. The entrance was difficult to find and very narrow once we got to it. There were large rocks jutting out. Kelp was everywhere. It was the most wild and uninviting place I had ever experienced.

Somehow we made it through the narrow entry, past the rocks to the cove. We were anchored in the small protected cove but could hear huge surf pounding on the surrounding rugged, rocky inhospitable shoreline.

One other sailboat tied up to a nearby mooring buoy called *Mandolin Wind* and had three older folks aboard. They were circumnavigating Vancouver Island. It was helpful to know that we were not alone in this wild and lonely place.

The night was windy, stormy, foggy, and rainy. There was a lot of pitching motion and the wind caused the diesel oil stove to smoke up again and fill the cabin. It took a while to clear the smoke all out by 02:30.

The next morning was stormy. We prepared properly this time: the water pressure, the stove, and the propane were off, everything was stowed, and hot water was put into thermoses. Everyone was dressed warmly with gloves, toques, rain gear, and wristbands. We all sat securely in the cockpit. Joshua took the helm for a while and everyone did really well. No sea sickness this time. En route we ate dry crackers. We could only motor, since we had a south wind and southwest swells up to eight feet high. It was very rolly.

Allan tacked out once and we got to sail for a little while. The motion under sail was much steadier.

LYDIA'S JOURNAL

Today we went from Sea Otter Cove to Winter harbour it was really wavy and the waves were like mountains and sometimes I could not see in front of me. In the Pacific Ocean it is wavy all the time and the swells are about 2 and sometimes 3 meters high.

Most of the five-hour trip was foggy but it cleared up by the time we got to Quatsino lighthouse. We motored into the Sound, straight to Winter Harbour. It is a very quiet, secure all-weather anchorage with a large government dock. We were able to tie up to the long spacious dock for free.

It was wonderful to go ashore and to be able to walk again. We hadn't done this for five days since leaving Port Hardy.

Winter Harbour is a well-protected large natural harbour. Years ago, it was an active centre for commercial fishing. When we arrived, there were only a handful of boats. The year-round population of Winter Harbour is eleven people. It is a desolate place and the weather is cold, wet and stormy most of the time. Interestingly it became one of our longest and most enjoyable stops of the entire year.

A special reward on this stop was a tour of the Coast Guard ship *Tanu*. *Tanu* pulled in to Winter Harbour for a day to replenish supplies of fuel and water. Our children were invited aboard the ship. "That is a real ship, Mom," announced Joshua. Joshua is passionate about boats. He had plastered all kinds of pictures of boats that he had cut out of magazines on the wall above his berth. In his mind, the bigger the boat the better. And *Tanu* was a big boat.

JOSHUA'S JOURNAL

A very exciting thing happened to us this morning. Last night, the Coast Guard ship came into Winter Harbour. Dad radioed the ship to arrange if we could have a tour in the morning. They said we could call in the morning. We did and they sent one of their inflatables to pick us up! We were given an awesome tour of the ship Tanu by one of the first mates. We met the captain. It was really neat!

He who lets the sea lull him into a sense of security is in very grave danger.

—*Hammond Ines*

CHAPTER 6

Close Call

We left Winter Harbour on a bright and windy day. The winds were strong at over 20 knots. We had a fabulous downwind sail for three-and-a-half hours to the very remote Klaskino Anchorage. Once inside the anchorage Allan started our motor, but discovered that we had no forward momentum. Reverse worked but nothing forward. There was lots of wind so we were able to sail to the mooring buoy in the anchorage. It was a little tricky, but we did it. Allan thought something was caught around the propeller. He did not relish going into the very cold water (less than 60°F) to figure out what was wrong.

The anchorage had four large mooring buoys. We secured to the first one, and Allan considered all of our options. We had minimal forward thrust but we had full reverse thrust. The propeller shaft did rotate, so Allan concluded that there was nothing wrapped around the shaft. It must be the transmission that was causing the problem. Allan decided we had to sail back up the coast to Winter Harbour, 27 miles away, to take the transmission out and get it sent as soon as possible to Vancouver.

JOANNA'S JOURNAL

Oh, great, we have a problem! Once at the Klaskino anchorage, Dad looked at where the propeller spins—not even working in forward. Dad checked the transmission and figured that that was the problem. What now! Mom and Dad started thinking up wild schemes such as "call a float plane—too expensive (of course Joshua would like that); carry on down the coast with no engine—too risky; go day and night down to Tofino—

too risky also; go back to Winter Harbour—that seemed the only possible scene." To finish that destructive day off we had delicious BBQed fish, and now it's the next day and I got real sick going back to Winter Harbour, so did Lydia!

The anchorage was very small, but quiet and well protected. We stayed the night and Allan's plan was that we would get up early in the morning before the northerly wind became too strong. It required sailing by tacking back and forth frequently to get through the long rock strewn narrow passage; an extremely challenging proposition. But we did it. It was a miracle that nothing disastrous occurred. We could have easily ended up on the rocks.

There was just the right amount of wind in the right direction. We left at 06:30 and it took us five hours to return to Winter Harbour in 12–15 knot NW winds.

I was thankful that Allan remained so calm and that he had the inspiration to get us back to Winter Harbour. Allan did not try to "shortcut" through the deadly nest of rocks. The same day, a boat in the next bay over from us, did get into the rocks and it was taking on water. Allan chose to go back the exact same way we came in. It was tricky enough since the passage was narrow and lined with reefs and rocks. We tacked back and forth many, many times, but slowly made headway out of the bay.

Once we got out of the bay, the NW wind was a perfect wind to sail by. We made a steady 6–7 knots going in the right direction. And the sun came out to cheer us on. This part of the trip I actually enjoyed. It was such a relief to be in safe waters away from the land. None of us noticed the rocking or rolling motion in the large ocean swells.

Joshua was a wonderful help. The three of us, Allan, Joshua and I worked in the cockpit. Tacking. Tacking. Tacking. Back and forth. Back and forth up the long passage. Quickly now! Keep on your toes!

"Ready to tack?"

"Dad, ready!"

"Going about."

We zig-zagged back and forth to our destination.

What a day. We were so grateful to be safe. I literally felt God's Hand of protection was upon us. The wind, waves and current were all with us.

We had a bit of concern about getting back up Quatsino Sound three miles to Winter Harbour. We had a little breeze that came up at the right moment in the right direction to push the sails. What a relief to arrive at the dock in such a short time. Allan had thought it would take us all day to get back to Winter Harbour. But, we were back before noon.

Allan admitted many years later that this situation was the most frightening for him that we had during our entire year away.

On arriving at the dock Allan immediately ran up to the telephones to phone the Vancouver transmission shop. He got the name of a mechanic in Port Hardy that could help with the shipping to Vancouver and arranged with "Frosty," a local resident (and the unofficial mayor) to take our transmission to Port Hardy. Allan and Joshua worked on getting the transmission out of our engine room. It took a few hours. The transmission was on its way to Port Hardy by 17:00. It had been a miracle day.

Now we had to wait.

Mandolin Wind arrived at the dock. They were the three older folks on the 30-foot boat from West Vancouver whom we had met at Sea Otter Cove. They were Gary and his cheerful wife Muriel, with their friend Harry. Gary and Harry had considerable experience with engines and transmissions and were able to discuss the finer points of boat mechanical systems. They were quite shocked that we had managed to sail out of Klaksino anchorage passage and back up Quatsino Sound without a working transmission. They were kind-hearted people in expressing genuine concern and care for us. Allan loves this kind of camaraderie and it represented the supportive boating community we would slowly become a part of.

JOSHUA'S JOURNAL

It was a cool day and overcast with a little bit of sun peeping through the clouds. Our family left the government wharf at Winter Harbour around noon. Winter Harbour is a secluded bay and small town, 30 miles south of Cape Scott. There was enough wind to sail comfortably in the rolling swell. Our destination was Klaskino Anchorage, an anchorage in the lee of an island, nestled against the rugged indent of a larger bay. It is so isolated that only knowledgeable navigators could enter through the maze of hazardous rocks.

Picture in your mind's eye, a white hulled sailboat with her sails up and five people in her cockpit, doing a good seven knots. We entered the channel that led through the maze of rocks. On the starboard bow was a small island with a lighthouse upon it.

Dad then turned on the engine, but alas, there was no forward thrust to the propeller. Questions started racing through our minds. We now had to tack back and forth through a dangerous channel. Not more than 100 yards off, huge breakers dashed onto the rocks, enveloping us in spray. No accident befell us on our way. It was very unnerving to tack between the rocks. There was sufficient current to push us towards our destination. We were now in total isolation.

Later that afternoon Dad checked over the whole engine and discovered that the transmission was not working properly. After a good rest we decided to head back to Winter Harbour under sail. We left the anchorage using reverse gear and then tacked vigorously through the nest of rocks, retracing our track from the day before. All I can say about that adventure is that it was cold and wet!

Just as we were nearing Quatsino Sound and the entrance to Winter Harbour, the wind changed in our direction and blew us up the channel. Until this time we had been beating into the wind with the spray flying across our decks.

The next few days were a lot of work in Winter Harbour, population eleven. Dad and I removed the transmission, had it trucked to Port Hardy and flown to Vancouver. It was repaired and sent back in a week.

My soul is full of longing
For the secret of the seamanship
And the heart of the great ocean
Sends a thrilling pulse through me.

—*Henry Wadsworth Longfellow*

CHAPTER 7

Waiting

We stayed in Winter Harbour for one week. It was a forced break for us. We had to slow down and settle into boat living. No longer were we trying to keep up the frantic pace we had been experiencing for years. The weather was dreadful all week. We had time to rest up.

Allan took the opportunity to get a great deal of work done on the boat. He installed our weather fax for satellite weather maps and our printer. He set up the lee cloths in our berths so we wouldn't get tossed around when trying to sleep during a passage. He fixed our antenna, so that our radio could transmit and receive to and from long distances. We became one of the few boats that had an extensive transmission range of a couple of thousand miles.

Allan had time to plan our itinerary. And most importantly we had a magical time with our children. It was so special because we didn't expect it in dreary Winter Harbour. That week became one of our best memories.

We developed a simple routine each day. The children would quietly get up early and begin their schoolwork without any prompting from us. We had breakfast then would go out for a walk, if weather permitted. We would have lunch, followed by a rest time on bunks and quiet reading. In the afternoon there was playtime for all of us. Since we had three dinghies, there was a boat for everyone. We had a small inflatable for rowing, a sailing dinghy that doubled as a rowboat, and an Avon with a motor on it.

Winter Harbour was like a small lake with plenty of room to row and sail.

Joshua and Joanna could each sail the sailing dinghy single-handed. They loved the freedom, quiet and exhilaration of flying around the little harbour in the gusty conditions. I tried it, but not very successfully. I had trouble telling which way the wind was coming from.

Joanna and Joshua had a natural and innate boat sense. It was wonderful to watch their competence improve each day. We had the large Avon inflatable with a motor that each of the children learned to operate. Joshua learned first and zoomed around the calm anchorage. He loved taking Lydia with him and going full throttle on the glass-like lagoon.

All three children were excellent rowers. We had two boats that could be rowed.

If the weather was bad, playtime was for games, working on the computer, or doing jobs with Daddy. We ate an early dinner, had reading aloud time, singing and prayer time, and early bedtime. We all had recorders, so we practised for our family performances. The children read a great deal on this trip. I packed on board 1,200 classic books. In all, they read about 100 books each, filling in a book report for each book written.

Winter Harbour is a dismal, grey place weather-wise even in the summer months. However, we enjoyed many of its benefits. Because of its isolation at the outer north end of Vancouver Island it is completely quiet. There is a huge dock with access to fuel and fresh water. It is a very secure place from storms. There are public payphones, a store with fresh produce, and a post office. Everything is there without the crowds or expense of a crowded marina. It is the ultimate Northern Vancouver Island experience, along with the 11 hardy characters that still live there. And we got to know them all. Frosty, the unofficial mayor, was very helpful and loved to come down to the dock and tell us stories. He happily received the homemade bread that I made in my pressure cooker. Michael was the postmaster and would come to the dock to see how we were doing. The owner of the store gave our children free ice cream. Fishermen frequented the dock and we would purchase fresh fish from them, as well as hear their stories. Sailing cruisers were continually coming and going. In this tiny corner of the world everyone has a story to tell and time to tell it.

A highlight for Joanna is a picnic. As our middle child, she is our creative romantic. We all went to the beach on the opposite shore across from the government dock. Together we collected dry firewood, made a fire (allowing one match), and roasted wieners and marshmallows. Joanna loves this. Each child had to find their own roasting stick and had to sharpen the point with a penknife. The lunch took three hours. Picnics became a favourite family activity for years later.

The sun eventually came out in this dark foreboding winter harbour.

Because we were in one spot for a week, the children got a great deal of schoolwork done. They wrote in their journals each day. What surprised me was that they all began to spontaneously write poetry. This was not something I had suggested. Poetry and creativity was an interesting result of getting away from it all and experiencing wilderness freedom.

Allan did read aloud time with our children each evening. Everyone would cuddle together in the aft cabin while I washed the dishes in the galley. It was magical for Allan and me to have this amount of prolonged quality time with our children. We will always remember those times fondly.

LYDIA'S JOURNAL

Today we did our school work and then I helped Dad set up the lee cloths. In case you don't know what those are their cloths [sic] tied up with string so that you won't fall out of your bed when we are night sailing and when we are healing [sic] over.

JOSHUA'S JOURNAL

O Canada, Our home and native land...

It's Canada Day; we're in Winter Harbour and I'm proud. Early in the morning, at about 07:30 Dad and I hoisted up our huge flag. Mom made a special breakfast of pancakes.

One thing had impressed us deeply on this little voyage: the great world dropped away very quickly... the matters of great importance we had left were not important... we had lost the virus, or it had been eaten by the antibodies of quiet. Our pace had slowed greatly, the hundred thousand small reactions of our daily world were reduced to very few.

—*John Steinbeck*

CHAPTER 8

Wildlife

We finally began to travel again; this time with a working transmission... or so we thought. We left Winter Harbour at 09:00 and arrived at Columbia Cove on the south side of Brooks Peninsula at dinner time. It was a long day for us and uncomfortable. The large ocean swells caused violent rolling motion in the boat. We had very little wind until we got to Brooks Peninsula where it picked up to 15 knots south/southwest. Tacking back and forth we finally managed to sail and the ride got smoother.

It was funny to see a huge sea otter floating leisurely on his back with his feet sticking up, looking totally comfortable and at home in the large swells. We saw quite a number of otters, especially around the kelp beds as they happily lay on their backs munching on crunchy sea urchins. Their look of total repose helped us to relax and take our focus off thoughts of sea sickness.

Offshore from Brooks Peninsula is isolated Solander Island. We saw puffins for the first time. They fly in large numbers above the steep island. They are so unusual looking. They are a northern sea bird with a brightly colored triangular beak. This is one of God's distinctively colourful creatures, found only in remote wild places.

Brooks Peninsula is a very large chunk of land that sticks out a long ways off of Vancouver Island. It divides the island into the north and south portion. Once we rounded Brooks Peninsula, the weather significantly improved and it got warmer.

We motored in to Columbia Cove. What a sublime spot. Kelp beds and fronds were floating everywhere in the bay. Eagles were soaring above us, surf and swell were minimal, and there was a shipwreck on the shore. There were no traces of civilization except for the shipwreck. Columbia Cove is a little bay tucked away ideal for refuge from the open ocean. Three other boats were anchored when we arrived.

Eerily, at dusk someone played the bagpipes as the sun set. In such remarkable and total stillness the bagpipes produced a haunting and mystical sound that added to the intense beauty and ruggedness of the place. The piper ended with "Amazing Grace." It was a perfect day sealed with a reminder of the Divine.

We spent a full day anchored in Columbia Cove. We hiked to the idyllic sandy beach on the outer side of land facing the open ocean. It is the most beautiful and untouched beach we have ever seen. It is not a long beach, but is stunningly picturesque with driftwood piled high on the shore, rugged rock pinnacles dotting the coastline, large green anemones hugging the rocks, starfish scattered in abundance in the tidal pools, and unusual large barnacles covering the rocky ledges. The colours and contrast of hue and textures on this beach are extraordinary. There is remarkable variety on this isolated coastline. It is rugged untouched beauty; natural and pristine.

We walked from one end of the beach to the other, then back again. We collected unusual shells, sand dollars, and rocks. We had a picnic lunch to Joanna's delight. This beach was another highlight of our trip.

And the stillness of the place was total. There was hardly any surf coming on to the beach as it is protectively tucked around the corner in the long shadow of Brooks Peninsula.

A sailor's joys are as simple as a child's.

—*Bernard Moitessier*

CHAPTER 9

Wild Places

The outside of Vancouver Island, in our opinion, is the most beautiful cruising grounds in the world. It is cruising at its best, because there is good wind for sailing and many protected anchorages. There is no need to make overnight passages, and there is a great deal to see and do. Five major sounds along this coastline can be thoroughly explored. It is quiet and tranquil. Utter wilderness. There are spectacular untouched beaches and a lot of wildlife.

There are few people boating on this coastline because it is so remote and you must be well equipped to attempt to navigate in these unforgiving open ocean waters. It's the ideal area to experience ocean sailing, without having to cross an ocean.

It was around Vancouver Island that we saw the most amount of wildlife and the fewest number of people, during our year away. It was during this initial six weeks of travel that we started to figure out *Morning's* mechanical, electrical, and rigging systems, and settle into the boating way of life. *Morning* had become our home.

Once we rounded Brooks Peninsula the weather improved. It was finally summer on the wild west coast and we made comfortable 30-mile day hops all the way to Ucluelet.

After Columbia Cove we visited the sublime anchorages of Petroglyph Cove, Rugged Point Park, Catala Island, Friendly Cove, and Hot Springs Cove. Along this pristine coastline we walked Hawaiian-like beaches, explored sea caves, sat in hot springs, and enjoyed downwind spinnaker sailing on sunny days. What a joy to share with our children the simple beauty of nature. Air, sea, trees, rocks, and wind combined into the onrush of scenery we experienced every day. It was healing and restorative. I call it the tonic of wilderness. Nature is a solace to any trouble one might have.

JOSHUA'S JOURNAL

Today was a gorgeous day. I had a wonderful sleep. For breakfast we had cereal and muffins. Joanna made both of these. We spent the morning doing schoolwork.

We left beautiful Columbia Cove around lunch time and headed for Walter's Cove, where we can pick up more transmission fluid for our leaking transmission! It wasn't fixed properly! We had a good sail and had lunch about 2 pm. When we were nearing the Cove we saw it was a real obstacle course with numerous red and green buoys marking rocks! When we got there we tied up at the government dock.

As soon as we tied up we went ashore and bought a lot of ATF for the transmission!

The days melted into one another.

The sea air was bracing and healing at the same time. It had a soporific effect on all of us, so we slept well every night. This was the only occasion on our trip that we had calm, secure anchorages every night. We were able to completely rest and relax after full days.

The entrances to these isolated spots were challenging, and were sometimes an obstacle course of hidden reefs and submerged rocks. We had to carefully follow our charts but the challenge of getting to these remote beautiful corners made it well worth it. I saw that this is analogous to life; complicated, but God has provided His chart, with markers and waypoints that can be found in the Bible.

Petroglyph Cove near Rugged Point is a tiny, little-known spot. It is nearly landlocked and is ideal for one boat to anchor in. It is well protected from all weather, and remarkably scenic. It is surrounded by beautiful old growth forest. A secluded wild place. It was tight to enter, but opened up into a little lagoon that was 30–40 feet deep. We ate our dinner on our deck watching five eagles chatter, swoop and dive for their dinners. We watched the birds for hours while we floated in total quiet. It is difficult to find the words to describe the beauty we saw.

Rugged Point Marine Park was a more open, exposed anchorage where we chose not to spend the night. We anchored there during the day so that we could go ashore and hike out to the open ocean beaches. There is a combination of very long, gradual beaches separated by a few delightful coves. We spent many hours walking from one end to the other. The children ran, leapt, skipped, raced, chased, beachcombed, dug in the sand, found quicksand, and darted in and out of the freezing water. Freedom. No people. Fresh sea air, spotless beaches. Paradisical (Joshua's own word). It was a perfect sunny day to play on an idyllic beach.

Catala Island sits at the entrance of Esperanza Inlet. We anchored off the sandy bight which protected us from the open ocean. We took our dinghy ashore, carefully motoring around the gigantic kelp heads which were the size of cabbages. There were a number of large sea caves to explore and disappear into. The children could imagine all kinds of adventures in this environment. In the bight was a beach covered with small, round, smooth rocks. What a rushing and smashing sound they made when even the smaller waves rolled in.

Friendly Cove is a more frequented anchorage because it is next to the Nootka Lighthouse. This light station is one of the most picturesque along Vancouver Island's outer coast. We had a tour of the lighthouse and met the keeper who had been there for 29 years. What a spectacular view and what a location.

Arriving at Friendly Cove had its challenges because it seemed to be a highway for small fishing boats. At the entrance to Nootka Sound the wind funnels into the area and our sailing speed picked up suddenly. We had our spinnaker up and we quickly exceeded our eight knot hull speed. We did not have a lot of control while trying to avoid a fishing boat that was coming directly towards us. We dipped precariously to starboard, almost touching the spinnaker to the water while we lost control of the rudder. We managed to get back on course when Joshua released our mainsail.

JOSHUA'S JOURNAL

After Friendly Cove we left for Hot Springs Cove. There seems to be a weather pattern that we have each day. There is usually 8 or 9 knots of NW or W wind in the morning rising to 16—18 knots in the afternoon.

Along the way, as we headed south, the weather continued to improve. Our challenge was to get around Estevan Point which, like Cape Cook on Brooks Peninsula, juts out into the Pacific. Rounding the point requires careful navigation.

The shoreline along this area is hostile and rocks extend more than a mile offshore. Estevan Point is flat, so the shore is not well defined and it can be difficult to see. The lighthouse at the point is the tallest along the west coast. It is 125 feet high and can be seen for 20 miles on a clear day. Reportedly, it was fired upon by a Japanese submarine in World War II, and has the distinction of being the only place in Canada ever under enemy fire.

Hot Springs Cove is the ultimate destination for most west coast cruising boats. The natural outdoor hot springs is a two or three kilometre walk from the wharf along a scenic cedar-planked trail that passes through thick rain forest. The boardwalk is famous for its planks carved or painted with the names and dates of visiting vessels. To arrive at the hot springs and to see the bubbling hot water flowing through several pools on its way to the ocean is an unexpected surprise. Our children loved going in and out of the ocean surf and into the pools and under the waterfall. It is nature's natural spa. The half hour walk to and from the hot springs made it all the more special for us.

Sailing to the south end of Vancouver Island, we followed renowned Long Beach, one of our favourite spots in the world. From our boat, however, we could not see it since we had to keep a reasonable distance offshore. When we anchored later in Ucluelet, we had a day trip to Long Beach. It is six miles long of hard-packed sand. The storms that pummel this beach have cast huge piles of driftwood on the shore. The enormity of the beach is breathtaking and great numbers of tourists can visit this beach, yet hardly be noticed. Our children ran and ran and ran on this long expanse of sand. A full day of walking, splashing and running around on this sandscape felt timeless.

JOSHUA'S JOURNAL

July 12: Once in Ucluelet Dad and I got the transmission out and we carted it up to a store with a Loomis service. It will be in Vancouver by tomorrow. This is the second time it is getting repaired! Since our sailboat was at the dock, we now had to move it out to the mooring buoy in the channel! Since we had no transmission, we used the dinghy to move our big sailboat over to the buoy!

July 13: We took a local bus to Long Beach. We walked on a loop through an old growth forest via a boardwalk. The forest contain Sitka spruce which fringe the shoreline only 100 meters deep since they need the salty minerals in the soil to survive. There was Indian paintbrush, licorice ferns, leathery polypody ferns, shelf fungi.

We then walked the beach, and had our lunch in the sand dunes.

The jewel of the wild places that we visited was at the southwest corner of Vancouver Island, called Barkley Sound. This beautiful sound is unlike any other on the BC coastline. It is 20 miles wide, 10 to 15 miles long, and sprinkled with hundreds of islands, islets, and rocks. These islands have large channels between them. The waters in this sound are unusually calm and dozens of anchorages can be found in the numerous nooks and coves.

It is a wild place full of sea caves, Indian middens, tidal pools, huge kelp beds, birds, sea lions, seals, tiny sandy beaches, and covelets; my word for tiny coves. Sea urchins, brightly coloured seaweeds, enormous mussels and barnacles, large green sea anemones, starfish, sun stars, kelp crabs, and dainty shells form a colourful rich sea bouillabaisse. The sea life here seemed oversized, even supersized from what we had seen so far.

The islands and islets are covered with dense forests made up of dwarfed, tough and gnarly trees. Sitka spruce is predominant. Bush whacking on these islets is difficult, so we spent our time on the beaches and waterfront.

JOANNA'S JOURNAL

A World of Kelp
Down in the depths of the sea;
where the otters live and be;
A forest of kelp,
extends itself,
Far beyond a rocky shelf;
that is where the otters dwell,
Floating and swimming in the rolly swell,
Eating and sleeping through-out the day,
Resting in kelp on a gentle sway;
Their feet in the air,
An elegant furry pair,
Spending their time grooming and washing their fur from head to feet.

We had a few delightful weeks in this area of the Outer Broken group doing lots of exploring. We went by dinghy so we could dart in and out of the small wild places quickly. We motored in our inflatable around Dicebox Island and Wouwer Island. On the outside of Wouwer was a small rocky islet covered with Steller sea lions. They appeared to be logs, tawny coloured and completely motionless. When we got close to them they began to move and bark. It was startling to see these massive sea creatures when they slipped into the water to check us out. Even though we were in our inflatable we did not linger to see what they would do as they approached us.

We were living in and experiencing a natural wilderness classroom.

LYDIA'S JOURNAL

Then we went out to the open ocean and saw huge rolly poly sea lions.
They were all making sounds that sounded like lions.

JOANNA'S JOURNAL

Waves
As they come splashing on to the rocks,
You'll see the geese fly by in flocks,
Over the sea,
Fighting those winds that whip up the waves
As big as can be.
The white little peaks that show at the top,
Because the wind won't stop,
On to the shore they come,
splashing loud on to the rocks.

Sea Breeze
I love the smell of the sea,
It feels so good inside of me.
I watch the gulls playing in the swell
It's worth a story to tell,
Of the birds and the horizon itself,
Far on it stretches like a watery shelf.
I live on the sea,
And the sea is part of me.

JOSHUA'S JOURNAL

July 17: We left for Effingham Bay on Effingham Island around 11 am.
The transmission is finally working and is dripping no transmission fluid!!
Halfway to Effingham, Dad started the watermaker. It produced very
good drinking water. We had some.

When we got to the Bay we anchored and rigged up the sailing dinghy and our two inflatables. Joanna went sailing and then Dad and Lydia went. Joanna and I were planing in the motorboat. It was deliciously fun!

July 18: Today was a very special day. Dad, Joanna, Lydia and I got up at 6:30 am and played Risk. I love this board game. We played until 9:30 am and had breakfast. Mom made pancakes and boy, were they good! After breakfast we went on an exploring venture. We took our Avon inflatable and lots of fuel. We went out to Dice Box Island with the sea cave and visited a rock off Wowser Island that had yellow, tawny sea lions. They are beautiful creatures. We went back to Dicebox Island and had our lunch at a sandy beach. We went and visited the sea cave on this island. We then hopped in the motorboat and went around Effingham Island. We went past the beach with the midden and abandoned village grounds. There was a sea cave there also, with ferns hanging across the entrance.

July 30: At last, it is sunny today! This morning I got up and did my diary. At 7 am I made muffins and cereal all by myself! I'm into being a cook! They were very tasty peach muffins! After breakfast we stretched our legs and went to visit the sand bar between Turret and Tricket Island and another island. We hiked all the way around Tricket Island and here I come to the exciting part...we were halfway around Tricket Island when we came to a narrow gorge, about seven feet high which sloped down to the water. It was too far to jump for everyone. Also, there was a gigantic sea cave. It was too slippery to climb around in front of the cave and up the other side. So we had to make a bridge over top of the water. We found some logs and placed them across. Everyone got across but as soon as I stepped off the logs they floated away with the tide. And I left my ball behind on the other side that Gram had given me!

The afternoon was spent cleaning up and getting ready to head for Neah Bay across Juan De Fuca Strait, tomorrow. How exciting! This is way better than staying in our house at Bowen Island!

The West Coast of Vancouver is a challenging stretch to sail, yet we enjoyed it thoroughly. There was lots to see and do. The distances between anchorages are short. The anchorages are the best anywhere; fully protected and quiet. The main challenge we had was dealing with a leaking transmission that had not been fixed properly the first time when we had spent the full week in Winter Harbour. Once we realized the transmission was leaking severely it became an incentive to sail as much as we could as we traveled down the coastline. Each day the northwest winds picked up by noon when we would leave our anchorage to sail southward. On arriving in Ucluelet we arranged for the transmission to be sent to Vancouver once again to get repaired. Consequently we had a full week in Ucluelet, tied to one of two large buoys in the centre of the inside bay near the town centre and main dock.

Ucluelet gave us access to Long Beach and the Federal Park. We also had visits from Gram and Grampa as well as special friend Phyll Elderfield.

When the transmission finally arrived and Allan installed it in place we quickly discovered it had been fixed properly. Thankfully we had no problem with the transmission for the rest of the year. Meanwhile, Allan became an expert in removing and reinstalling the transmission which was a tricky and very awkward operation. He had to wrestle it in and out of position which was difficult to do on his own.

Allan's patience in dealing with mechanical equipment was a key part in a having a successful trip.

UNITED STATES

23
24
25
26
27
28
29
30
31
32
33
34
35
36
37
38
39
40
41
42
43
44

If the boat started shaking we stayed on course and didn't lose focus. That made the difference.

—Sebastian Vettel

CHAPTER 10

First Overnight Passage

Neah Bay, Washington was our jumping off spot for the 168-mile journey to Astoria, Oregon, 30 hours away by sea. This would be the longest nonstop stretch of time on our boat and our first over-night passage. We had to round Cape Flattery, then head south along the Washington coastline. This stretch becomes a dangerous lee shore when bad weather develops.

We spent a few days in Neah Bay to prepare for the trip. We sailed each day in Juan De Fuca Strait practising sailing with our harnesses on, experimenting with different sail configurations, including our staysail and storm trysail, and we practised heaving-to. We tried leaving and anchoring under sail. According to Joshua we were running the "Peters sailing school." Everyone did a lot of winching, which is to get sails into position by pulling the lines or ropes in around the large winches in the cockpit. The gusty Juan De Fuca conditions gave us good practice.

JOANNA'S JOURNAL

I'm so excited. You can probably guess why, too. Well, maybe not. By now after all this babble in my journal you ought to know that we are going off shore to San Francisco, by means of short overnight trips. I'm excited about it!

We finally left the dock. We prepared everything we could think of. Our things were carefully stowed away. I prepared food that was easily accessible.

Thermoses were filled with hot water. Harnesses were out. We placed rain gear close at hand. The children prepared to play their parts and stay tucked in cosy corners of the boat while we were underway at night. Lee cloths were set up inside the cabin. Hatches were tightly closed.

We prayed.

The first 12 hours underway were dream-like. We had the cruising spinnaker up and the wind was an ideal 10–15 knots. However, later on in the evening the wind picked up over 20 knots, and then died completely. This is the fickleness and unpredictability of the ocean environment.

The seas were now sloppy and the conditions uncomfortable. It took time for Allan to figure out the best combination of sails. He realized we had to have the sails up and the motor on at the same time to maintain a reasonably comfortable motion. Sailors typically do not like to motorsail. But, once we started, the motion on the boat improved considerably.

A serious problem developed when our boom kept slamming uncontrollably back and forth in the steep swell. We had lines to restrain the boom but they did not keep the boom completely still. The violent motion put severe strain on the bolts holding our boom to our mast.

Joshua and I took the 18:00–22:00 watch. We had our difficulties; especially trying to figure out the direction of a freighter that we were convinced was coming towards us. Its green light was showing meaning it was actually moving to the left of our vessel. With the messy ocean swells we were easily disoriented.

When it was Allan's watch from 22:00–02:00, he had the challenge of dodging huge, well-lit fishing boats. Where were their nets? Did the captains see us? Where should we position ourselves? In the midst of this boat traffic a thunder and lightning storm developed. We had never been on the water during a lightning storm. And for small boats this is the worst and scariest situation. For three-and-a-half hours Allan worked hard to avoid the dark squalls and lightning strikes. A strike can wreak havoc on a boat's electronics. It was a horrible and very tiring night.

We did the best we could with watches, but we needed Allan a lot for changing sails, starting the motor, checking our position, etc. At different times in the night everyone felt queasy with the lack of wind and sloppy seas.

Allan calculated that we should arrive at the Columbia River entrance by 07:00. And we did. This was unexpected, since our speed, direction and course were extremely erratic.

JOSHUA'S JOURNAL

Today was a very exciting new adventure for us! We left for Astoria at 5 am. Joanna was on watch with Dad. It was very foggy, cold and wet morning. We didn't even see Cape Flattery because of fog. I got up at 7 and we were still motoring. We had watery gruel for breakfast. We put the sails up and sailed for the rest of the day.

For supper we munched on peanut butter sandwiches, sipped V8 juice, crunched on crackers and cheese and nuts, and chewed vegetables. And the sun came out and we sailed in perfect bliss. After dinner I had a rest and Dad and Joanna put the spinnaker up.

After supper we saw two huge grey whales come very close to our boat. One actually jumped out of the water and landed on its back. Most amazing. We were about five miles off of the Washington coast. I was on watch with mom from 6–10 pm. Mom and I saw many fishing boats and freighters in the dark night. I slept pretty well all night!

We had no trouble coming up the Columbia River. It is notorious for being a difficult bar to cross. We found out later from the U.S. Coast Guard that this bar is the most dangerous in the world.

We traversed the bar successfully while motoring past a lot of fishing boats and two huge freighters.

It took four days for us to recover from this challenging leg of travel. We wanted to be fully rested before continuing south to Newport, Oregon. It would be a 125-mile trip and another overnight at sea.

This was also our first introduction to pelicans. They are unusual birds with gangly bodies, long beaks, and wide wingspans. They seemed to be everywhere. They cover the docks and sometimes land on boats making a dreadful mess with their sticky excrement.

JOSHUA'S JOURNAL

August 7 and we are in Astoria. We have done a lot of walking in this old historic town. Today we caught the Astoria Riverfront trolley that was actually used at the beginning of Astoria in 1913! We got off at the maritime museum and I had a wonderful time there. It had all the history of the Columbia River and all the ships that were wrecked. We learned about the New Carissa from Panama that went aground in Coos Bay. A freighter that had to be blown up and sunk in Feb. 1999. We saw hundreds of model ships and tons of old articles from sunk ships. There was lots of scrimshaw which is whale bone carvings that the sailors would do in their spare time. Then we went to visit the Lightship Columbia. This ship sat at the entrance of the river on her anchor marking the entrance. It is now a museum that you can visit.

If you cannot arrive in daylight, then stand-off well clear and wait until dawn. After all, that's one of the things God made boats for—to wait in.

— *Tristan Jones*

CHAPTER 11

Help!

Allan calculated that the leg from Astoria to Newport, Oregon would get us to the harbour entrance by 01:00 if we left Astoria at 05:30.

Leaving Astoria was more challenging than when we entered it. The Columbia River is a reasonably wide channel and has a lot of shipping and boat traffic coming in and out. This morning the fog was thick and it was difficult to see anything. We had to rely on our radar, which was confusing to read because we were close to shore and could not differentiate all the objects showing up on our screen.

Allan chose to leave on the "wrong" side of the channel, so that we didn't have to cross the wide channel at the harbour entrance in front of all the traffic.

Allan was accurate in his calculations of our arrival time to the Newport Harbour entrance. However, we made the unwise decision to enter the harbour at night. This is one of the cardinal rules of cruising: never enter an unknown harbour at night. In retrospect, we realize this was a huge risk to take and it resulted in a terribly close call.

Once we crossed the Columbia River bar and re-entered the Pacific Ocean, we had a steady 20 knots of wind that peaked at 28 knots. This is a lot of wind, but ideal for a good consistent sailing speed.

We tacked down the coastline following Allan's course line of 10–15 miles offshore. This became our preferred distance from shore down the U.S. coastline. It gave us enough sea room from shore yet some inland protection from the larger seas further out. This distance kept us well inside the freighter traffic, but outside the fishing pots placed closer to shore.

It was a bouncy rough sail, but we made good time. It was an exciting trip. It became foggy and as nighttime approached there was lightning over the Cascade Mountains. The thought of lightning kept us vigilant and on our toes. We did not relish the thought of a wild night in a lightning storm. Thankfully, the storm did not reach its fingers out to sea and we avoided another ordeal.

I took the late night shift and was surprised by the number of birds in the air swirling around our boat. I could not see them in the dark fog but could hear them with their weird calls and sounds. Some seemed to squeak, cry, purr and whine, sounding like human babies or cats. It was an eerie feeling. Night passages were a new experience for us, so the night sounds were disconcerting.

Our boat produced a bright highway of phosphorescence. It was exhilarating to turn around in our dark cockpit to see a well-lit trail extending far behind us.

It was foggy at the Newport Harbour entrance. This was not a good thing. The wind had increased and it was raining heavily. The conditions were becoming more and more difficult. Allan realized it would be dangerous to try and negotiate entering the harbour. He radioed the U.S. Coast Guard to ask for help.

The Coast Guard responded quickly. Allan told them that we had never sailed these waters and that we had three children on board. The Coast Guard offered to escort us in to the Newport Harbour.

It was challenging to follow their boat into the harbour because it was difficult to see and follow their lights against the background of city lights. With the huge ocean swells, both of our vessels were bobbing up and down at different times and we would frequently lose sight of them. It was completely disorienting to be in this unfamiliar place in the dark.

We gasped when we saw how tight the entrance had become. We would have never found that small opening on our own. A large dredging operation almost completely blocked the entrance to the harbour.

We were escorted into the marina to our dock. It was close to the entrance of the harbour. We still could not differentiate city lights from any of the navigation lights or dock lights. Everything was bright, glaring and very confusing. Once we docked, we were overwhelmed with relief. It was a huge wave of emotional and physical release we felt the instant we stopped moving.

This was our "hairiest" (Joshua's expression) experience yet.

We were exhausted.

Eric, the captain from the Coast Guard boat, politely came aboard, had us sign forms, checked our emergency equipment, and told Allan he was a good captain.

We could have hugged this young man for literally saving our lives. We gave him and his crew cookies, Canadian pencils, and postcards of the Rockies. He was delighted with our small gifts and warm reception. We were deeply grateful for his expertise, experience, and courage.

It was sobering to think that this level of public naval rescue service is not available in most of the rest of the world. We began to seriously question how would we fare when we left American waters and were completely on our own. This was a thought to consider since Mexico would be our next destination.

We were only two months out on our adventure and we were already seeing a purposeful Providential Hand of protection. This experience was one of many more that we would go through. As we headed further south, the challenges became more frequent and difficult. The years of preparation sailing back and forth across familiar Georgia Strait, British Columbia in all kinds of conditions, paled in comparison to being out on the open ocean.

For me, this realization was deep and profound. I was not the sailor on board. Consequently, I felt the most vulnerable. I was ever conscious of supporting my husband as well as being the best mother I could be for our children, so that they would all have a positive experience during our travels. But the reality of what we were doing was starting to sink in. My faith became my lifeline.

...over the breaking billows, with bellying sail and foaming break, like a flying bird...

—*Beowulf*

CHAPTER 12

Harbour Hopping

The northern U.S. coastline is a challenging dangerous lee shore for the length of Oregon and Washington with long distances between places of refuge. Watching weather patterns is vital. Almost all the harbours have bar entrances where timing the tides, currents, sea conditions, and daylight is critical to be able to make an entrance.

For six weeks we harbour hopped down to San Diego, sailing or motoring 10–15 miles offshore. We enjoyed destinations such as Astoria, Newport, Coos Bay, Crescent City, Eureka, Fort Bragg, Bodega Bay, San Francisco, Monterrey, Morro Bay, the Channel Islands, and our final U.S. destination, San Diego. The further south we travelled, the weather became warmer and the ocean swells were more consistent and moving in our direction of sail.

This turned out to be an excellent part of the trip with a lot of good sailing. The largest amount of wind we experienced was 35 knots of wind, but overall we experienced the idyllic 10–20 knot sailing breezes. This meant that Allan frequently put up the spinnaker. Or he put out the mainsail on one side and the gyb on the other side (wing-on-wing). Both configurations worked well for downwind conditions. We had many pleasurable stops. With our children on board we felt it was important to make it an enjoyable, memorable, and positive trip. We wanted the overall experience to be life-changing, character-building, and fun.

While the majority of cruisers make the five-day jump from Victoria directly to San Francisco or the seven-day leg directly to San Diego, we decided to harbour hop down the coastline. This is not as commonly done, but it gave us time to enjoy a lot of fascinating places. It was also a lot more relaxing. We were able to hone our sailing and navigational skills. Going in and out of harbours, crossing bars, and avoiding boat traffic made us learn to work with our radar, carefully read our charts, plot our position, and thoughtfully plan our itinerary.

And most importantly, we were starting to work well together as a family team. We realized we needed one another. For example, Joshua, who was keen throughout our trip, was developing excellent sailing skills. He was a remarkable asset, and could work quickly with Allan. He was totally at home on the water and in boats. It was second nature to him. He had no fear. He was positive and enthusiastic about everything we did. In his mind the difficulties we went through were all part of the grand adventure.

Then there was our dear Joanna. By this part of our trip she was writing copious amounts of poetry. When sea conditions got rough, she and Lydia would bounce in the cabin and pretend they were riding horses and jumping them, which both did later in their teenage years. If the conditions were really rough they would lay in their bunks and practise Morse code on each other's backs. Remarkably creative, Joanna thought of activities for her and Lydia to do during the long days of sea travel. Joanna loved working in our kitchen cooking meals and helping me. She, like Joshua, was also totally at home on the water and in boats.

Lydia, our youngest, was more tentative on the entire trip. However, she had Joshua and Joanna to follow. She was not alone, and we cuddled her throughout the trip. She astonished us later as her confidence in the water and on the boat rapidly improved. It took about seven months to achieve this but the transformation and maturation was inspiring to watch.

Increasingly, we were also meeting more and more cruisers and others who were helpful, generous and who went out of their way to encourage, assist and advise us. Probably the couple who remain dearest to our hearts are Roy and Winona on their boat *Saucy Lady*. Like us, they also chose to harbour hop down the U.S. coastline, so we felt like we were given two angels to travel with us. Our itineraries were not exactly the same, but we kept bumping into each other (not literally!) at marinas and anchorages. It was always a joy to see them. Winona was the miracle woman who could bake cakes or pies from scratch while underway on the ocean in a small boat. To attempt any kind of cooking underway was a skill I never developed... or at least for which my stomach was not prepared. More than once, Winona would have a multi-course dinner ready for our entire family on their boat when we arrived in a common destination. They are remarkable people. And Roy could fix anything. Allan was handy, but Roy helped Allan reach another level of skill. We were so thankful to meet them.

There were many highlights on this stretch of travel. We learned to anchor in open ocean anchorages. This was a foreign concept to me. How could it be both open ocean and an anchorage? This sounded like double talk. Port Orford, Trinidad Head, and Shelter Cove were all stops we made. It was pretty weird for us to continue to rock and roll all night after rocking and rolling all day while underway. Sleep did not come quite so easily. We realized how spoiled we had been by the wonderful, calm protected anchorages around Vancouver Island.

We enjoyed a number of stops enroute. For example, the stop at the Redwoods near Crescent City was amazing. This stately kingdom of gentle giants is magnificent. We went on short hikes through the well-marked trails in the forest. The sand dunes at Bodega Bay were expansive, and we walked for hours while overlooking the ocean. Passing under the Golden Gate Bridge is a memory I will never forget. San Francisco is considered the starting point of "dream" cruising. I made that term up, and it means cruising becomes pleasant and enjoyable from this point on. We enjoyed a couple of fun days in San Francisco; walking, travelling on the bus, going to museums and art galleries. It was a bit of a shock to be in a large metropolitan city after three months of comparative isolation.

JOANNA'S JOURNAL

We are travelling again, this time from Crescent City to Trinidad Head. It was a little overcast but we didn't mind that. I did all the chart plotting and the log today. That was fun. Me and Dad learned lots of new stuff with the GPS this afternoon. That was fun, too.

Today our destination is Eureka, only 20 miles from Trinidad Head. I spent the hours in the cockpit looking around at the sea birds: pelicans, puffins, cormorants, and gulls.

Oh boy, that was close! At first we thought it was a log, but no, it was a sleeping whale!! We came so close to the humpback whale that we could see the barnacles on his back and that was neat.

At Monterey we visited the world-class Monterey Aquarium. We got to see close up the sea life that we were living with. The jellyfish display was unusual and very beautiful. We had seen thousands of jellyfish during our three-hour sail across the bay from Santa Cruz to Monterey. To see them under coloured light in a dark room gently pulsating in their huge tank felt mystical. We loved the deep-sea canyon fish display tank and there was an open air tank full of skates (a large flat rhomboidal fish) that we were able to touch. It was all incredible.

LYDIA'S JOURNAL

Today we went from Eureka to Shelter Cove. We anchored and had spaghetti dinner. After dinner we played recorders (me and Joshua) and we had yogurt and Inka and sang songs that Joanna had learned on her recorder and Dad played with her while the rest of us sang. What a family night!!! In the night me and Joanna went outside and looked at the night sky. It had no moon and a ton of stars. We saw two shooting stars.

Shooting Stars
Shooting stars are so bright
On a warm summer night.

Shooting through the sky
Quicker than a fly.

With the moon in sight
the stars are always bright!

When the night is almost done
And the shooting stars are done their fun

And dawn is near
the shooting stars will fade they fear!!!

The sail, the play of its pulse so like our own lives: so thin and yet so full of life, so noiseless when it labors hardest, so noisy and impatient when least effective.

—*Henry David Thoreau*

CHAPTER 13

Rigging

Rigging is the most critical system on a sailboat. We certainly had our challenges with it. At Port Hardy it started with our furling mainsail sticking. Just before we left home, Allan had coated the sails seams with a UV protector that left a slightly sticky residue. So, pulling the sticky sail in and out became a frustrating arduous task. We got the answer for that dilemma in San Diego. Our friend and fellow Canadian, Dave Dobson, a sail maker, told us to coat the entire mainsail with baby powder. After an excursion to Costco, I bought a case of Johnson's baby powder so that Allan could liberally coat the sail. After that we had no more trouble with our mainsail sticking.

Travelling from Newport, Oregon to Coos Bay, California we had two uncontrolled gybes. A controlled gybe is something sailors often do while sailing downwind. A gybe changes the boat direction until the sails swing across the boat. An uncontrolled gybe is not planned. The main sail will violently swing across the boat taking the boom with it, and the boat can quickly lose control and direction. It is very dangerous and has to be the worst experience for the sailor since it compromises the entire rigging system and things can break. In our case, a pulley suddenly snapped off the boom as it swung wildly across to the other side of the boat. Fortunately Allan was able to do fast fix-it work and the boat was stabilized. We were able to continue sailing.

The toughest day of constant stress on our rigging was during the 70-mile hop from the open anchorage at Port Orford to Crescent City, California.

Allan observed that the boom-vang (a tackle system that restrains the boom from lifting) was unattached and a lot of bolts on the boom were loose. Allan was able to fix it just in time before the wind really whipped up. Under strong winds the whole thing could have broken and the boom would have detached from the mast. We would have had no mainsail. Allan was becoming intuitive about checking every part of our boat continually. *Morning* was a large, complex working machine and she needed to be meticulously cared for, as she was certainly serving us.

On this particular stretch to Crescent City we did some serious sailing in strong winds and big seas. Our rigging, which was completely new when we left home, was getting a considerable workout as we had already travelled 1,500 miles. We started out early in the morning enjoying an idyllic 10 knots of wind with the spinnaker up. By noon the wind picked up to 18 knots. We got the spinnaker down, fast. The wind continued to build up to 27 knots and the seas were getting large, lumpy, and confused. The boat handled well especially when we reefed the sail, making it smaller. Our GPS indicated that we were going 9 knots, which is well over our usual 7 knots of speed. Our boat was really moving and becoming harder to steer.

By St. George Reef, just outside of the Crescent City harbour, the conditions were very rolly. We were making excellent time so Allan kept as much sail up as possible: a partially furled mainsail and a partially furled gyb. We were thankful to have furling sails, which meant we could do everything from the cockpit. Going up on deck to get sails up or down would not have been easy. Allan had no problem handling the boat by himself because the rigging was efficiently set up and the boat was correspondingly responsive. With her deep fin keel and skeg mounted rudder, *Morning* was well designed to power through most seas with stability.

This was one of the rare occasions that Allan chose to hand steer. Hand steering is not something you do on ocean passages because it gets very tiring. But large waves were coming astern of us and it felt like we could get swamped at any point. By hand steering Allan moved the boat quickly, dodging the gigantic cresting swells.

I did the unimaginable and accidentally hit the automatic pilot switch off with my elbow. Later, Allan became tired and wanted to stop hand steering and change over to the automatic pilot, but it seemingly did not work. Since we were offshore sailing it is very important to have the autopilot system operational. This was a second possible disaster in a few hours. I was horrified. When I realized what I had done, it was a relief to turn the switch back on and have the autopilot working. After the difficulties we had with our transmission on the west side of Vancouver Island, we did not need another important system breaking down.

We neared Crescent City by about 18:00. There are impressive reefs and rocks off Point St. George. Castle Rock is huge and jagged. We were being bounced around so violently it got tricky keeping track of our exact location. We used GPS, radar taking repeated latitude and longitude positions to find our exact position on the chart.[1] The waves settled down just as we approached the boat basin and entrance. We put on the engine and brought the sails in. The wind was still strong, so we had to be vigilant in our approach. The buoys were easy to see and we had no trouble. We were thankful it was clear and sunny.

At the dock we learned from other boaters that the fishing fleet had come in early because the conditions were too rough for them. And we were out in it! We were grateful for a strong boat. The new rigging was severely strained most of the day yet it held together. That day turned out to be one of our wildest and longest sailing days.

[1]GPS in the 1990's only gave latitude and longitude without any map.

The pessimist complains about the wind; the optimist expects it to change; the realist adjusts the sails.

—*William Arthur Ward*

CHAPTER 14

Holding

The wind was steadily climbing to 35 knots. I saw the knotmeter read 37 knots, which is about 62 kilometres per hour. At this point I stopped looking at the knotmeter. These were the most extreme wind conditions we experienced in our entire year away. Allan retained good control of the boat and *Morning* sailed beautifully over the huge waves. The Nordic sailboat is designed to sail in these conditions. It was exhilarating and Allan was enjoying himself immensely. We had to take turns hand-steering since we were afraid to overwhelm our autopilot. It was fabulous sailing in the Californian sunshine. It was a startling contrast from the dark, drizzle and fog we had experienced further north.

We had no problem getting to the Bodega Head whistle buoy, although we had one or two very steep waves (12 feet or higher) that caught us unawares. These large waves had the unnerving effect of lifting the boat high in the air and then spilling and rushing over themselves sending the boat flying downhill. It almost felt like the waves were going to fill the cockpit, but *Morning* gracefully went up and down with each surge.

As we neared land the swells began to abate. I realized I had to trust the boat even though the ocean looked very scary and overpowering. We sailed into Bodega Bay with the wind a steady 34 knots. We had to tack then reef the sails quickly.

The gyb flapped wildly as we furled it. There was a lot of strain on our sails, sailing into the wind, close-hauled. Spray was going over the boat and we were getting soaked. We managed to haul the sails in. We started the engine, but motoring directly into 34 knots of wind was slow going while being pitched around. The boat moved forward at 2 knots. Allan was nervous about entering the riprap jetties to get to our marina destination. The wind could easily blow us to one side or other on to the rocks. Just before reaching the jetties our engine mysteriously cut out. With a few seconds to think, Allan and Joshua rushed forward on deck to free the anchor into the water while yelling directions at the rest of us. The anchor grabbed hold and dug in. It set in 35 feet of water and held us firmly. We were not moving at all but we were within a minute of being dashed onto a surf-pounded rocky shore.

Joshua yelled at Allan, "That was great Dad! Let's do it again!" This shout summarized Joshua's experience of our year sailing. He had no fear. It was always, "Dad, I just love this...let's do it again."

Our anchor held.

I had no thoughts of "doing it again."

Our hearts were pounding at this close call, but Joshua was thrilled with the excitement of it all. He was a huge part of our success in getting the anchor off the boat quickly. Our family team unit was working well together. Survival depended heavily on each child doing their part.

Allan radioed the Coast Guard to alert them that we may need assistance. He checked the engine and bled the air lock out of the fuel lines, caused by our pitching around. He tried the engine again. It started! Relieved, we motored through the entrance to Spud Point Marina. The Coast Guard was preparing to come out to help us, but we were able to confirm with them that we had working systems and could safely make the jetty entrance on our own power.

Calling on the radio to the marina, we were given instructions to enter a specific slip. Before we knew it we were safely and securely tied up to the dock. So much had happened to us in a few hours. The unpredictability of weather and ocean kept us sober and made us grateful for a safe arrival.

We stayed in Bodega Bay for a couple of days to recover from exhaustion. Little did we realize that this was a small sample of what we were to experience in our year ahead.

LYDIA'S JOURNAL

Big Fluff Clouds and the Great Grey Sea and the Storm

Fluff white clouds roam on the sky as we go by
The great gray sea lay flat beneath us
Seabirds flying, whales jumping
As the clouds are dumping lots of rain
As the sea goes choppy and stormy and the winds gain.
We fly back home because we know that we are in for a big, big
STORM!!!

JOSHUA'S JOURNAL

Sailing from Fort Bragg, California we had a fresh breeze and it was
getting stronger by the minute. We were sailing wing on wing, with a
reefed main sail and gyb. As we rounded the point of Bodega Bay, the
wind freshened, verging on a gale. We had a lot of difficulty hauling in
the sails. We had to run up into the wind with the huge waves and spray
dashing over our boat and drenching all of us. Everyone was straining
at the winches including me. It was tough. It had been a lovely day for
sailing though.

We had to start the engine because the wind was on our nose as we
turned into the very narrow entrance. The boat was having a hard time
making headway. The wind was now blowing 35 knots. Suddenly cough,
splutter, and the engine died. Dad and I flew to the bow and down went
the anchor. I think this was just to prove that a CQR anchor can hold in
very strong winds!

We made an urgent call on the radio to the coastguard. They offered
to send us their 44 foot lifeboat to tow us in. Dad replied and said that
we would try and start the engine first. In the tossing and heaving of the
waves, Dad went into the engine compartment and bled the fuel line. The
engine then started! Our fuel tank was one third full but still had allowed
air to enter the intake for one brief moment. We pulled in the chains and

pointed our bow for the breakwater. It was difficult in the chop but we arrived safely into the channel. In passing the coastguard station we gave them a grateful blast on the horn. We headed for the marina and were very glad to tie up to the dock. It was a great learning experience.

Off Cape Horn there are but two kinds of weather, neither one of them a pleasant kind.

—*John Masefield*

CHAPTER 15

Five Capes

Cape Scott, British Columbia
Cape Flattery, Washington State
Cape Mendocino, California
Cape Conception, California
Cape Corrientes, Mexico

During our one year at sea we learned that large points of land that stick out into the sea mean something. These are the capes, and they have a serious reputation with sailors. This is where the weather is accentuated, terrible things can happen and nature can be in her wildest mood. These points of land typically separate significant areas of climate and terrain change. These are areas of extremes. The exposed nature of these points of outstretched land can seem like formidable barriers to any yachtsman approaching them for the first time. I felt a huge sense of accomplishment and relief every time we rounded a cape, as did our entire family. We had proven something. We had reached a new level of expertise

Our first major cape was Cape Scott at the northwesterly point of land on Vancouver Island. It is a place where weather conditions can suddenly change for the worse. We heard that winds can change direction and rise from 5 to 45 knots in less than an hour. Combined with the sea conditions, especially when the tide changes and the tidal stream is opposing the wind, terribly steep waves can develop. Many worthy vessels have sunk in this area. During winter months during a storm, seas can reach frightening heights, some of the highest in the world.

After rounding Cape Scott, we ventured for our first time into the open Pacific Ocean. So it was a significant cape for us to round, and was the demarcation for the beginning of our offshore travels.

Cape Flattery is the northwestern most point of the United States. It is on the corner of the Olympic Peninsula where the Strait of Juan de Fuca joins the Pacific Ocean. There is a lighthouse and a tall rectangular rock on the west side of the cape that looks like a giant pillar. This is a distinctive prominent point, which once we rounded felt there was no turning back. It was a downhill ride all the way to San Diego, downwind sailing for 1,000 miles.

Cape Mendocino has a notorious reputation as the classic turning point for southbound sailors. It is located just north of San Francisco and is the dividing line between the cold, foggy, more challenging Northern California coastline, and the summery, mild, idyllic Southern California coastline. This is where "dream sailing" begins. Cape Mendocino sticks out the farthest west on the U.S. coast. The North American continent cuts in a significantly easterly direction after this point of land. Even freighters and large ships are very wary around this section of coastline. Sailors give it a wide berth since it has the reputation of waves that sometimes build up to 30 feet for 100 miles out.

Cape Conception is another significant point of land separating *sunny* Southern California from the *sunniest* part of Southern California. It too is treated with respect and we watched our weather window very carefully. We went around the cape at night and we had a good quiet trip with calm seas. It was an 18-hour motoring trip from Morro Bay to Santa Cruz Island in the Channel Islands. We were shocked at how much warmer the weather became after we rounded Cape Conception. It was also the last time we experienced any fog or rain for the year. Our warm weather gear and rain gear were put away. T-shirts, shorts, and swimsuits became the norm. For the next nine months of our trip we experienced perpetual summer.

After rounding Cape Conception we noticed a significant increase in the number of cruisers out on the sea. While our conditions were excellent for getting around the cape, we did not expect such a dramatic increase in boat traffic. The lights on the ocean increased, starting with the huge oil rigs offshore. These looked like giant lit up birthday cakes on the water and could be seen for miles.

The other lights were on the freighters. By this point we were in major freighter shipping lanes. It was startling to see how quickly the freighters would move. We learned to always get behind a freighter and to never get in front of one. We had heard enough stories of freighters running over small boats without seeing them.

The last important cape adventure was rounding Cape Corrientes just south of Puerto Vallarta, Mexico. It is called the Cape Horn of Mexico. We did not think it nearly as daunting as the other four capes, but we still treated it with caution. Interestingly, of all of the capes we rounded, Cape Corrientes turned out to be the most challenging for us because there was a lot of wind.

We rounded Cape Corrientes on Christmas Eve heading south for our favourite anchorage of the year, Tenacatita, a 24-hour trip. We left in the morning on December 24, a cool cloudy day which should have given us a clue for what the weather would be. We experienced serious winds, up to 35 knots. Fortunately the waves were not huge at 6 to 8 feet high, but it was very rolly. We pulled in some of our sails early on because we watched the barometer nose dive 7 millibars in 6 hours. This amount of sudden drop in the barometer was scary.

The barometer is an important instrument for the sailor because it shows the atmospheric pressure that can indicate the slightest change in weather. This was a sign that the weather was rapidly deteriorating. We were sailing, actually surfing, more than hull speed all day until midnight. We stayed on the radio to try and ascertain the conditions that would be up ahead. Only one woman responded to us on the radio since everyone else was occupied with Christmas Eve festivities. She was a cruiser and gave us specific directions on how to safely enter Tenacatita Bay at night. As I pointed out earlier, entering an unfamiliar harbour at night is one of the last things a sailor wants to do. We would be (again) breaking a cardinal rule of seamanship.

I will never forget that wild dark night of flying through the water. Since we were getting quite far south, darkness suddenly descended at 18:00.

Dusk was not long and lingering like at home. For six dark hours we were careening down the Mexican coastline. The trail of phosphorescence behind the boat was spectacular as it formed a brilliant highway behind our boat. Our bow wave was lit up as well and the effect was startling. Everything around us was aglow.

We were making such fast time that we were concerned about arriving at Tenacatita in the dark. We did not want to enter any harbour again at night. But once we were well clear of Cape Corrientes and its vicinity we had only 8 knots of wind until we arrived in Tenacatita in the morning. This was our last overnight passage for many months. We had made a total of 15 overnight passages and were ready for a good rest, and it was Christmas Day!

The rounding of these capes marked a significant transition in our sailing ability and confidence levels. Now we were facing the decision, whether we would consider making the three week crossing from Mexico to the Marqueses in French Polynesia. Allan's ultimate dream was to circumnavigate the globe. The boat was well-proven, but were we? This was the question we began seriously asking ourselves for the next six months in Mexico.

The art of the sailor is to leave nothing to chance.
—*Annie Van De Wiele*

CHAPTER 16

Fog

Fog is one of the most potentially hazardous weather conditions. It often lies in a long bank close to shore. We experienced fog during our first three months of cruising, and none after we rounded Cape Conception in southern California.

While we experienced a lot of light fog around Vancouver Island, we did not experience anything really heavy and thick until we reached Barkley Sound at the south end of Vancouver Island. We had anchored in a charming little cove called Turret Bay and had it all to ourselves. We had a couple of very quiet and 'puttery' family days enjoying a campfire on the beach, exploring tidal pools and sea caves, and cleaning and packing up for our next leg of our trip, heading down the U.S. coastline.

On the morning of our departure across the Strait of Juan de Fuca we woke up to the sound of men's voices calling out to us. We climbed out to our cockpit and were astonished at the sight of four large, loud men in a small, open, run-about boat that was sitting low in the water.

It was a very foggy morning. In fact it was the thickest fog we had ever experienced. We could not see the shore less than one hundred feet away and we could not see anything else but this little boat floating next to us. It was an eerie feeling. We were out in the middle of nowhere and these men wanted directions to the nearest town. They had absolutely no idea where they were. We couldn't believe they managed to get through past all the rocks to where we were anchored. We were in the centre of the Outer Group of the Broken Islands, which was a very long way from anywhere.

How did they get to this obscure little cove? Had these men been out all night? They looked like they could have been. It appeared that there was alcohol being consumed and we did not see much evidence of proper equipment (ie. life jackets, food/water, lights, warm clothing, rain gear). Their boat was so low-lying in the water that one wave could have easily swamped them. Allan attempted to give them our latitude and longitude so they could get a bearing, but this information didn't seem to resonate with any of them. So Allan gave them some simple instructions on the general direction to Bamfield and they trustingly tootled off. We were aghast. It was unbelievable for us to think that anybody would be so totally unprepared in such a remote area.

When fog rolls in, the surroundings take on a surreal, mystical appearance. Islands will drift in and out of view and the line between sky and sea vanishes. It is a world of grey. If the sun is out just above the fog, the intensity of shades of gray are constantly changing. Looking through the vapour curtain is an experience all in itself.

Leaving Fort Bragg in California was foggy, but we went far enough away from land to get out of it. We skirted the massive fog bank that hugged the coastline. We had hours of motoring alongside it before the fog dispersed when the winds picked up.

JOSHUA'S JOURNAL

This was a very sunshiny day. We left Shelter Cove with Saucy Lady in bright sunshine. Today is a motoring trip. Around lunch time we saw two porpoises riding our bow wake. That was pretty neat. I played the recorder and I am getting good at it. I love music and I sure miss the piano. There was a lot of fog along the coast but we stayed out in the sunshine. Saucy Lady stayed in the fog! We had our rest and then arrived at Fort Bragg. The entrance was very very narrow and it wasn't foggy anymore!!

Motoring under the Golden Gate Bridge on our arrival to San Francisco was a somewhat disappointing experience because we could not see much of the bridge. It was encased in fog and we could only see the lower 50 feet or so.

An early start to a very exciting day!! I can't believe I'm actually going to see San Francisco! It was another motoring day in dense fog. We got to the entrance around 11:30 am. The Golden Gate Bridge could barely be seen because of a dense fog layer. I could only see the span of the bridge. It was very exciting! In San Francisco Bay the fog dispersed and we saw the Alcatraz Island with the renowned federal state prison that is now a tourist attraction. We saw many famous buildings along the waterfront, ferries, car freighters. We went under the Oakland Street Bridge (no fog). It was a double decker bridge! I saw the Ghirdhelli Square, Pier 39 and Fisherman's Wharf.

San Simeon is a small open ocean anchorage just south of Monterey, California. About 15 miles before we arrived at San Simeon we ran into thick fog. We could not see the top of our mast and sitting in the cockpit we could not see the bow of our boat. This was very thick fog. It felt dense, almost claustrophobic. We were completely surrounded by it. We had to totally rely on the GPS and radar. It was a good exercise in using our instruments. We came into the bay using our instruments until at the last minute the fog cleared up enough for us to see the little bay, a dock and three small boats anchored. Then the fog completely enveloped us again.

While anchoring, a bright cloud and lightly coloured rainbow went directly over our boat. It was as though God was speaking to us, telling us we were not alone and that He was watching over us. This was a great comfort to us.

Our 85-mile hop from San Simeon south to Morro Bay was a motoring trip on glass-like seas. It is Morro Bay that is ranked as the foggiest place on the West Coast. It has a very tight entrance that doglegs around the impressive landmark of Morro Rock. We experienced no fog coming in or going out of Morro Bay. We were very fortunate since this is typically a cold and foggy location. It would be an ordeal to navigate through the Morro Bay entrance in bad conditions.

JOANNA'S JOURNAL

Now today is worth writing about! All morning we walked the dunes of Morro Bay. It was lovely. With the sandpipers that have those long beaks and spindly legs. They are so cute! And the waves, what waves! As they gently run up the sandy beach. When the day was over we invited Roy and Winona out for dinner at a Chinese Buffet. It was so, so, so good!

They that go down to sea in ships
that do business in great waters,
These see the works of the Lord,
and His wonders in the deep: Psalm 107

....

A collision at sea can ruin your entire day.
—*Thucydides (5th century BC)*

CHAPTER 17

Sea Traffic

There was a steady stream of sea traffic in Georgia Strait (ferries mainly), a small amount of traffic up Johnstone Strait, and virtually no boats on the outside of Vancouver Island. We saw freighters going in and out of Juan de Fuca Strait, big fishing boats travelling down the Washington and Oregon coastline, and substantial freighter traffic from San Francisco to San Diego. We saw virtually nothing along the Mexican coastline, with the exception of one cruise ship and one ferry.

Once we got to Southern California we saw the giant oil rigs offshore. At first we had no idea what they were since they looked like small cities floating on the water. But freighters were the expected challenge and we were vigilant in staying as far away from them as possible. What we didn't expect was to be on collision course with other sailboats. This happened on two occasions.

The first time was after we rounded Cape Conception. *Saucy Lady* was travelling with us but we lost sight of them once night fell. We had been at a constant speed on a set course steered by the autopilot for several hours. At 02:00 a sailboat was getting close to us. I thought it was *Saucy Lady* coming over to say "Hi" which is not really a wise thing to do, nor is it very good seamanship. I soon realized it was not *Saucy Lady* but a different boat. Since

I was on watch I woke up Allan and we radioed the boat. It was a vessel called *Chez Moi*. They quickly answered. The wife was on watch and was quite confused with our heading towards their boat.

Meanwhile, we thought they were heading towards us. They had been on autopilot at constant speed for several hours, headed towards Santa Barbara and now they crossed right across our path. We simultaneously changed our courses and continued underway. We got far too close to their vessel. This was a weird experience because we were miles off the coast in a huge expanse of ocean where we could not see another light anywhere. Meanwhile, *Saucy Lady* and other friends heard our conversation on the radio and wondered what on earth we were doing. No one had heard of such a thing. Two sailboats on collision course? None of us had heard of that happening. Lesson learned; you never know who or what you will meet on the open ocean. There are always unexpected surprises.

LYDIA'S JOURNAL

We saw lighted oil rigs and one that had a flame on it and we also saw porpoises and dolphins. That night we rounded Point Conception which can get up to forty knots of wind and very big waves but when we went around it at night so it was very calm in fact it was like glass. We went with Saucy Lady and they had a good night, too. We dodged a few freighters and talked with a few people on the radio.

The second time we were on collision course was when we were heading north after spending many months in the Tenacatita area. We were returning north back to Puerto Vallarta and I was on watch from 22:00 to 04:00. In retrospect that was too many hours on watch and I was too tired to think clearly. I saw two lights approaching us. I stared and stared and stared into the night. My brain was thick. What did the lights mean? What color were they? It seemed to take me ages to ascertain that there was a white light on top and a green light on the bottom. My brain was still thick. The boat, with the white and green lights, seemed to be coming straight towards us. I couldn't think. Too tired. Eyelids thick. I just wanted to sleep.

But I had to do something and I did not want to wake Allan. I finally decided to turn starboard when I should have followed the rules of the road and not turned at all or turned to port. The boat passed by us, again quite close. The crew on that boat must have wondered what I was doing. There was no radio contact and we both carried on course and quickly disappeared apart from one another in the night. In a sleep-deprived state my judgement was poor and sluggish. I put our entire family in danger. I was deeply shaken. My only consolation was that I didn't hit the boat and I didn't wake up the family.

Some years ago—never mind how long precisely—having little or no money in my purse, and nothing particular to interest me on shore, I thought I would sail about a little and see the watery part of the world.

—H. Melville, "Moby Dick"

CHAPTER 18

Open Ocean Anchorages and the Channel Islands

Open ocean anchorages do not make a lot of sense to me, even having experienced them. Instead I would call them "open ocean shallow places where you can throw down an anchor and rock and roll all night." They are not restful places, because you are always aware that if wind or sea conditions change you have to get up very quickly and reset the anchor or move somewhere else.

At these anchorages I seemed to sleep with one ear open. I was always aware of the sounds around the boat. I was the one that would hear the anchor chain scraping rocks all night. Often I would imagine we were dragging anchor or any other worse scenario I could think up.

The ultimate open ocean anchorages are in the Channel Islands off the Californian coast. Some of the anchorages have very strange names. Names like Forney's Cove (who was Forney?), Prisoner's Cove (yup, one could feel imprisoned in that tight cove), Coches Prietos (should we know what this means?), Albert's Cove (Albert who?). Most of them barely had room for more than one boat, so I could not figure out why they were called anchorages. I was not impressed with any one of them. And predictably we rocked and rolled all night.

The Channel Islands are unusual outcroppings of bare land and rock. The coves we stopped at for the night were very scenic and beautiful, usually lined with a delightful beach. But swell and surge was high so we had to anchor very, very carefully. Getting on and off the boat to shore was also a challenge since we had to get through the high surf.

The Channel Islands are 8 islands 60 miles away from the 18 million people on the congested Southern Californian mainland. They are worlds apart from the mainland. Few people actually visit these islands because they are difficult to get to. Because we could sail there, we benefited from their isolation, quiet, peacefulness, and remoteness. The northern five islands make up a National Park. They are Santa Cruz, Santa Rosa, San Miguel, and Santa Barbara. We only visited Santa Cruz. The other three islands outside of the park that are more southerly are Santa Nicolas, Santa Catalina, and Santa Clemente. We visited Santa Catalina.

These islands are remarkable. By visiting them, we were glad to avoid the busy Southern California coastline until arriving in San Diego. So, apart from a brief visit to San Francisco, we stayed in remote and wild places for the first three months of our trip.

The Channel Islands are home to over 2,000 plants and animals of which 145 are found nowhere else in the world. It had the feeling of being a "Galapagos-type" island American version. We loved our few days on Santa Cruz and the populated Catalina Island, but anchoring conditions were not ideal, so it was necessary to head towards our final U.S. destination: San Diego.

We motor-sailed around a lot of Santa Cruz Island where the guidebooks suggested there are about 15 anchorages. We checked out many of them: Cueva Valdez (too exposed), Fry's (nice, protected, tight but had too many boats), Pelican Bay (also crowded). We ended up for an overnight at Prisoner's Cove which was named the favourite by the author of our guidebook. It was not too exposed so the motion on board was not uncomfortable. The highlight was that we were near a lovely beach which we walked in the afternoon. The children loved the beach and were very quick to start making dams and sand castles.

We tried to visit the world-famous Painted Cave, but realized there was too much wind, swell, and surge. The Painted Cave on Santa Cruz is one of the world's largest known sea caves. It measures 1,215 feet in length (more than four football fields long), has a 160-foot tall entrance, and is almost 100 feet wide. We idled our boat for a time and even got our dinghy off the boat to see if an entry into the cave was feasible. Sadly, we had to forego the attempt. Doing things right is often just not doing something wrong.

JOANNA'S JOURNAL

Today we set out with Saucy Lady to go inside the Painted Cave, the biggest Sea Cave in the world! I was so excited! Well, anyways the weather wasn't as calm as yesterday. So we couldn't do it. Oh well! But I've made up my mind to visit that cave someday! We practically went around the Island of Santa Cruz. Each bay or cove we looked into was either unprotected or too crowded!! But finally we stopped at Prisoners Cove. It is quite a picturesque place. We went ashore in the inflatable without much problem.

We motorsailed to the south end of the island to Coches Prietos, which refers to the black pigs we saw there. It seemed like an ideal anchorage at first glance, giving the impression of a tropical island with its turquoise water and white sand beach. There was only one other large boat near there. Some experienced cruisers who knew the area well told us to get aggressive with our anchoring technique at Coches Prietos, so we followed their advice. We had been told to get close to shore to anchor so that it would almost feel like our stern was on the beach. It was a little unnerving to do it. Especially with the swell breaking all around us. The surge was lifting us rhythmically up and down three to four feet and large waves were crashing on the nearby beach a hundred feet away. Our friends on *Saucy Lady* anchored out deeper.

We went ashore for the afternoon, walked the beach and let the children swim in the surf, in their wetsuits. They loved it. This was the first time on our trip that we had really spent any time playing in the ocean water. Joshua built a huge sand castle on the beach.

At the same time a new challenge awaited us. We were getting a lot of sand in the boat. Sand in a boat is not a good thing. We had to become meticulous in keeping it out because otherwise it gets into everything, including the bilge pumps.

We had a reasonable night going up and down in the swells. We put out both a bow and stern anchor to keep from getting broadside to the waves.

We got up early for a walk to the high bluff overlooking the bay and ocean. It was quite a steep scramble, but we made it, following pig runs. We saw two small black pigs and one giant sow.

The view from the bluff was spectacular. We took some photos of our lone boat in the bay. It was an unnerving sensation to watch it bobbing up and down in the swells. Allan was thoughtful, then with alarm announced that he was really uncomfortable watching our boat bob up and down so vigorously, looking like it could be slammed on the beach.

We scrambled down the hill, jumped into our Avon inflatable and timing our departure through the surf, got back on board and quickly pulled up the anchors. The surge and swell had significantly increased. We had to back up even closer to the crashing surf to pull up the stern anchor over the transom; then we pulled forward to pull up the bow anchor. This was a new way of anchoring for us and we experienced an adrenalin rush in the execution of it all. We managed a quick exit.

Around the bluff there was a cove that was far more protected. Two other sailboats were already tucked into Albert's Cove. We pulled in beside them, lowering the stern anchor and then pulling the bow forward on the bow anchor to tighten everything up. It was a relief to be in a calmer location.

We let the children go ashore on the tiny little beach. The children swam. While drying off on shore a little piglet came up to Lydia! Lydia was startled and didn't know quite what to think or what to do. But Lydia is our animal lover and this new friend delighted her. The piglet followed the children around and as I watched from our anchored boat I could see how pleased they were. From my perspective, however, I was getting nervous about the prospect of an angry sow showing up unexpectedly. She did show up later after the children left the beach.

The next morning we left Santa Cruz Island at 05:30. It was a 68-mile motoring day to Santa Catalina Island. We had no problem getting the two anchors up. Pulling the stern anchor first over the transom; then ahead to retrieve the bow anchor. We were slowly figuring out our anchoring strategies which were part of learning new sets of skills on each section of the trip.

There was very little swell on this leg. Perhaps there was some protection from Point Conception or from the Outer Channel Islands. It was a lovely trip. The highlight on this day was seeing large dolphins frolic around our bow wave for a good hour. Joanna was by herself at the bow enjoying the entire hour, hence her poem.

We saw a lot more boats as we approached popular Catalina Island. Now we were only 22 miles west of Los Angeles. Catalina is quite a barren looking place, much like Santa Cruz, but drier and steeper. We enjoyed the well-protected Catalina Harbour on the west side of Santa Catalina Island. There was a lot of room for boats to anchor. We anchored fairly close to shore and Allan put out the stern anchor. We were settled by dark and snuggled together in the cockpit to enjoy the warm evening. Finally, we were in a warm place and a very calm protected open ocean anchorage.

The next morning we set sail to go around the south end of Catalina with our destination of Avalon on the other side of the island.

At the point when Allan had all the sails up with the spinnaker pole on the gyb, the wind increased to over 20 knots so it was time to reef. For the first time, we practised heaving-to with various sail arrangements; an important storm tactic. We continued to sail downwind, with a small gyb (reefed) and small main (reefed). It was a very comfortable ride.

The wind died down when we turned the corner to go north to Avalon. Coming into Avalon we saw an open anchorage packed with mooring buoys and boats. Behind this huge parking lot of bobbing vessels was the picturesque little European-like town of Avalon with its distinctive Art Deco building on the point.

To come into such a crowded area of anchored boats was overwhelming. We met a harbour patrol boat who directed us to an anchor buoy. It was tight quarters with a brisk wind and chop but we managed to gingerly pick up our assigned mooring buoys at bow and stern without smacking into the boats tight beside us.

This was another first. To be lined up on double anchor buoys with hundreds of other boats in a small area was something we could not even imagine. This was not a marina. It was a giant floating parking lot. Who knows what would happen in high winds and high seas. I imagined what a mess it could be if everyone tried leaving at the same time.

JOSHUA'S JOURNAL

When we came into Avalon anchorage we were amazed at all the traffic, boats and ferries. There are 264 mooring buoys and packed with boats!!

This was the end of our season in open ocean anchorages for the time being. It was excellent preparation for our seven months in Mexico. Meanwhile, we would have the next six weeks in San Diego preparing the boat before leaving for Mexico.

JOANNA'S JOURNAL

Dolphins I Once Saw
I once saw such elegant creatures,
With such majestic features;
They were Dolphins!

I watched them play for an hour,
They splashed sending water up in a tower;
They rolled to look me in the eye,
I heard them talk and sigh;
Oh those Dolphins!

They jumped high into the air,
I watched, amazed, around me the day was fair;
Their eyes were beady and black,
I saw a yellow scratch on a Dolphins back;
Oh those Dolphins!

Their backs were grey and their stomach white,
They splashed their flukes' with all their might;
They swam so fast, as quick as a flash,
Sending up a welcoming splash;
They got me wet,
But I was the happiest person you have ever met!

LYDIA'S JOURNAL

When we were in the Channel Islands (Santa Cruz) we stopped at a lovely
bay with a nice beach. We saw three little wild pigs that were running
around. Soon the swell would get too large to stay in our anchorage
Coches Prietos, so we went around the corner to a more protected
anchorage which was called Alberts. We decided to have a swim at the
beach. We rowed ashore in the surf and started swimming. I decided to
play in the sand with my back towards the hills. In a few minutes Joanna
and Joshua (my brother and sister) started yelling at me. I turned around
and saw a baby pig sniffing me. I was really surprised! We decided to
leave and swim at the boat because the Mother of the pig would be upset
if she came. The little pig stayed with us until we left and was quite sad
when we did leave. Joshua had actually petted the little wild pig. Long
ago people brought pigs to kill the rattlesnakes. There are no rattlesnakes
now, but lots of baby pigs!

We went back to the boat in the surf. You can't really time the waves when
you get out so you just have to get wet.

JOSHUA'S JOURNAL

Getting close to San Diego we saw a huge aircraft carrier, army helicopter and submarine!! The sub passed quite close to us. We rounded Point Loma and pulled the sails in. Our first view of San Diego!! We're here already! We passed the San Diego Naval Submarine base, where there were 5 subs and huge frigates. San Diego is the only major naval, army, and air force base, next to Honolulu on the West Coast. Pretty neat! We tied up to the police dock and got checked in. It only costs $5 per night!

Photo Journal

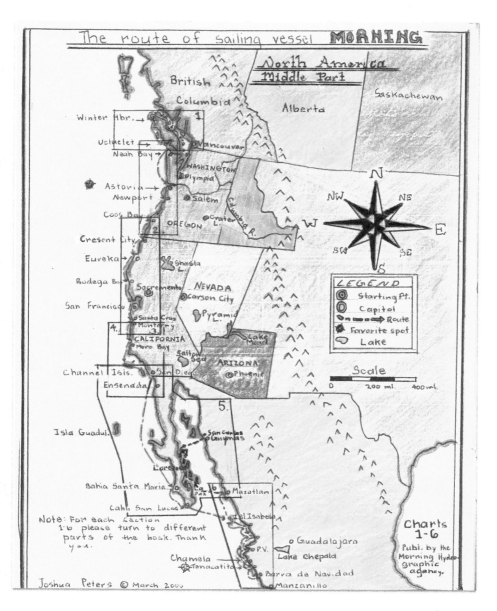

ABOVE The trip, from Joshua's journal

ABOVE Family photo in San Diego
FACING Messy business: fish caught while sailing down the west side of Baja
BELOW Joanna and Allan playing recorders while motoring down the USA Coastline

ABOVE Chacala, a wonderful beach at our first landfall in Mexico
FACING Crossing the Sea of Cortez and a feathered friend stopped by to visit
BELOW Joshua playing soccer with school children in Chacala

ABOVE Chacala elementary school class
BELOW A fun day exploring La Cruz in Banderas Bay

ABOVE Joshua solo sailing in the Tenacatita Bay
BELOW Joshua receives certificate of thanks from Neener 3

ABOVE Raft-up celebration for the manta ray rescue heroes, Tim and Joshua
BELOW Barre de Navidad lagoon: motoring back to Morning in our Avon inflatable

ABOVE La Manzinilla: fresh groceries in Tenacatita Bay
BELOW Allan, Lydia, Joshua, and Joanna with a typical Mexican panga at Chamela

ABOVE Relaxing in the Nuevo Vallarta marina
FACING Our children with local school children in Nuevo Vallarta
BELOW Agua Verde, Sea of Cortez on the east side of the Baja

ABOVE Lydia with her "find" in Ballandra Bay on Isla Carmen, Sea of Cortez
FACING The pants that fouled our propeller in Mazatlan
BELOW Hiking above the anchorage in San Juanico

ABOVE Coronada Island fishing bonanza

ABOVE Conception Bay fabulous cactus!

I've met the most interesting people while flying or on a boat. These methods of travel seem to attract the kind of people I want to be with.

—*Hedy Lamarr*

CHAPTER 19

Camaraderie

Our first stop in San Diego was at the police harbour dock for three nights. San Diego is an expansive harbour with a huge amount of shipping traffic. For the first time in our lives, of which we had many on this trip, we saw submarines and aircraft carriers. Joshua was breathless seeing such a variety of ships and vessels that were military and non-military. Loud oohs and aahs came from the cockpit from Joshua, as he sat perched for hours on one of our large winches. Boats have always fascinated Joshua and he was mesmerized by all that we saw.

We had been away from home now for three-and-a-half months. We were getting into the groove of being on the boat full-time as a family. We had routines and activities. The children had school work and lots of projects they made up on their own. The girls did hand sewing with fabric I bought, learned Morse code, worked on their journals, made artwork, wrote poetry, play acted with their stuffed animals, wrote summaries of the highlights of the trip so we could send these to friends and family, played board games, read books, wrote up their book reports, and wrote postcards. They were always happy to help us where they could.

Joshua was Allan's right hand man and was up for any adventure with Dad. Joshua thrived on some quiet time too, and worked hard on his school work. He wrote extensive journal entries and magazine articles, pored over boat magazines, read a copious amount, and learned how to run some of the basic systems on the boat, specifically the radio.

We were fortunate to find moorage slips in a variety of marinas throughout the San Diego harbour area, which gave us the opportunity for rest and recovery time as well as for some creative fun time. Everyone was productive and happy.

While Allan kept the boat running, I made all of the meals, cleaned and organized our tight living space, helped the children with their school work, kept everyone on schedule, did more cleaning, organized shopping trips for groceries, wrote lists, kept a detailed journal, wrote and mailed our family newsletter (to family, friends, and Allan's clients), kept careful track of our food storage, cleaned, checked in on the radio, organized get-togethers with other cruisers, made a lot of food, kept in touch with family at home, worked really hard at keeping everyone from getting sick, planned fun activities, and encouraged everyone to work together and get along, and cleaned. I was the non-sailor on the boat, and did my best to try and catch up to learn about the many systems on board.

I was happiest in San Diego, because it was easy to get off the boat, see lots of people, and get anything we needed. For me, to be at a marina dock for an extended time was pure joy. No more rolling around. No more motion. Easy access to shore. And lots to do on shore. One significant highlight was getting our mail and email. I loved keeping contact with everyone we knew and met.

The San Diego Harbour had numerous large marinas. We stayed at a number of them. It also meant we had access to an adjacent hotel with a pass to the beautiful swimming pool. We swam in it every day. We could enjoy warm freshwater showers as well with as much water as we wanted. To simply stand under the warm shower was pure heaven for me. It was three months since we had had that luxury. And I knew it might be the last time for a while.

We began to feel quite human again, stepping out of survival "roughing it" mode.

The next six weeks went by quickly. We were very busy during that time, especially Allan who was determined to fix everything that he could think of. He started by fixing the boom attachment by refitting more bolts, fixing all the leaky pipes and pumps in the boat, doing some rewiring, taking apart and greasing all of our winches (a huge job), coating our main sail in baby powder periodically so the furling main could easily slip in and out, replaced the head, set up the wind vane, photocopied additional charts, oiled and cleaned up our woodwork, fixed our skylight seals, refreshed our batteries, flushed out our cooling system, collected spare parts, and checked out our inflatable tenders for leaks. Allan worked steadily and carefully attended to the myriad details on the boat. Our trip was a success because of his focused, disciplined, careful approach to boat preparation.

The highlight for us in San Diego were the friends we made and cruisers we met. We were introduced to the cruising community on Wednesday mornings at 10:00 at the Downwind Marine Store close to our marina area. We arrived in San Diego one month earlier than most cruisers, so we had a good month to work and prepare the boat without much social distraction. Work first, play later was our plan. As folks began to arrive, we were able to take the time to visit, share meals and do things together.

We arrived in San Diego September 15. Other cruisers arrived mid-October. We met them as they all started to check-in daily on the radio. It was the cruiser's net on channel 68 at 08:30 Monday to Friday. We loved answering roll call, and soon became a familiar boat name to many. *Morning* was a straightforward simple boat name and people remembered us.

Because there is a shortage of moorage in San Diego, we had to get creative in figuring out where to stay. We were fortunate to have a one month stay at the Shelter Island Marina when we first arrived. That was where we were able to focus and get a lot of boat work done. We had another stay on the police harbour dock, then Kona Kai Marina, Chula Vista Marina (miles south at the end of the harbour), La Playa Anchorage, A-9 Anchorage, and the Silver Gate Yacht Club. Because we belonged to the Bluewater Cruising Association in Vancouver, we got reciprocal visiting privileges at the Kona Kai and Silvergate.

Everywhere we docked or anchored we met more cruisers and made more friends. At the police dock the Canadians started to arrive mid- to late-October. We started to bump into more and more people that we knew. We shared ideas, itineraries, plans, boat preparation tips, sailing experiences, and generally we felt we had accessed a wonderful wealth of information from folks. We love learning from others, and this proved to be a huge asset in many of the decisions we had to make.

The grand finale in San Diego was a giant family picnic put on by Downwind Marine Store. There is a large beach area where the Downwind staff set up barbecues and tables to provide free hamburgers, hot dogs, and drinks for everyone. All the cruisers brought salads, chips, or desserts. It was a fabulous and varied buffet. We had our lunch and dinner there, were the first to arrive, and the last to leave. Our children loved every minute of the time. This was community at its best. There was lots of good food to eat, people to visit with, children to run around and play with. It was wonderful to have so many friends all together in one spot before we separated on long legs of travel south.

LYDIA'S JOURNAL

Here is our routine list in San Diego:

MORNING	1.	read
	2.	breakfast
	3.	schoolwork
	4.	lunch
AFTERNOON	5.	rests
	6.	swim
	7.	showers
EVENING	8.	play
	9.	dinner
	10.	go to bed

JOANNA'S JOURNAL

Note: Joanna wrote six detailed pages about our family and my parents visit to Sea World and the San Diego Zoo. Sea World was her favourite and she was delighted with the trained whale and dolphin shows, the walruses, otters, belugas, penguins, puffins, and the bird show. She ended her entry with:

Sea World has the best playground. We played on it until we had to go. We also enjoyed a root beer float. We had dinner out. I had Grilled Shrimp. That was one of the best days of my life!

I am getting excited now as we talk more and more about Mexico and the South Pacific. I am thinking way back to when we were living at Grams' house, before we left Bowen Island, and what a long ways we have come! You might not want to hear the same thing over and over every day so I'll write a list of what I do even though you might already know:

-wake to blue sky at 6:30–7:00 am
-brush my hair and get dressed
-have a look at the world outside
-get started on my journal
-eat fruit
-a little school work
-have breakfast
-Math, Spanish, Language Arts
-lunch, finish at 1:30 pm
-read until 2:30 pm
-go for a walk/swim or just hangout
-dinner
-teeth
-read
-sing/recorders
-to bed

Today, October 25, went without a fault. Mom said that everyone was hyped about going to Mexico. Well, I sure am! Debby on Echoes of Summer (motor yacht) said that Mexicans will love my blonde hair. She said I could make friends easily! How lucky I am to have blonde hair! This life is great! It is so much better than sitting around at school. Speaking of school though, I had better get working.

Today, October 26, was rather exciting! We began with school work as usual. Sharon from s/v Poets Place gave us her book of poems. This is where the excitement begins. Sharon (a poet) has a 14 year old friend named Bonnie. Bonnie lives back in Washington. This Bonnie wrote a letter telling about herself and gave the letter along with a stuffed bunny to Sharon to take on her cruising trip. Bonnie said to Sharon that if she found a good writer, to give the stuffie and the letter to that the person so they could be Bonnies' pen-pal. Sharon picked me!

November 1: Wow! We've almost been out for half a year! This morning I woke up to a golden sunrise, beautiful crimson sky. Someday I'll write a poem about it!

November 4: At dinner time our boat seemed so friendly and cosy. It made me think of home! We lit a lamp on the table, the lights turned low and the music playing. "we've had to live for 6 months on the boat for it to get like this!" Mom announced!

November 9: Dad bought T-shirts and baseball hats to trade in Mexico. I tell you I jump at the very word "Mexico"! Because it's another winter to skip. Christmas is coming and my 12th birthday on Feb. 6 will be a warm one!

JOSHUA'S JOURNAL

We are getting ready to leave San Diego for Mexico! We still do the check-in on the radio each morning. Downwind Marine has a roll call and its fun to listen to it. I worked on my Spanish course for the rest of the morning. I have my own little place to do my schoolwork.

This sounds really silly but Dad and I put baby powder on the mainsail! This is to get rid of the stickiness produced by the water based seam sealer. It only took a half an hour to do!

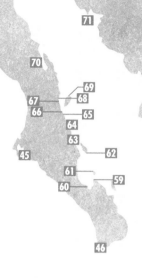

MEXICO

If I take the wings of the morning or dwell in the outermost parts of the sea, even there shall Your hand lead me, and Your right hand shall hold me. Psalm 139:14-16

....

Men in a ship are always looking up and men ashore are usually looking down.

—*John Masefield*

CHAPTER 20

Faith

It took faith to leave San Diego. We were going to leave the familiar and very comfortable extensive San Diego harbour. We had thoroughly enjoyed the camaraderie and amenities of this world class shipping destination. Entering Mexico we would be on our own.

I was nervous. Excited, but nervous.

The children were ecstatic.

Allan was ready for the big adventure to finally begin.

I was actually really nervous. I knew I could not sail the boat on my own if I had to. I did not know all the systems on the boat. I certainly couldn't fix anything. I could barely operate the radio. I wasn't sure how we would do with boat travel for days on end. I was afraid of everyone becoming seasick.

I prayed.

My one consolation; we were together as a family. I loved this part the best.

We made our departure at noon on Sunday, November 14. Many of our cruising friends came by in their dinghies to say goodbye. We were one of the first boats to head south. It was after hurricane season now and Allan felt all of our systems were working and ready for lengthy sea travel. We wanted a head start of the rest of the cruising fleet because we did not know how many stops we would make along the way.

Allan decided we would make a four-day non-stop trip to Bahia Magdalena; a huge open ocean anchorage three-quarters down the Baja coastline. This was our longest leg of travel. In total, we would travel 1,000 miles from San Diego to Puerto Vallarta. We would discuss our next travel plans to points south once we had arrived in Puerto Vallarta.

This first section would be our longest stretch of time without getting off our boat.

It was a really scary thought to leave all that had become familiar and comforting to us in delightful San Diego. We could get any boat part, have wonderful camaraderie with fellow cruisers, have the convenience of buying food and any supplies we needed, and we could enjoy all the luxuries that American society offers. The ease and comfort of living would dramatically change as soon as we left the USA. Access to weather information and to Coast Guard assistance would be something we would leave behind. We would be on our own for the next seven months with all the concerns of maintaining our complicated boat systems and maintaining the health and well-being of our three children.

That takes faith.

We would be entering another country and, to us, foreign waters. While Allan had lived in Mexico for four months as a Rotary exchange student after Grade 12, I had never been to Mexico before. This was also the first time for the children to visit a country very different from home. This would be a totally different type of challenge; the cross-cultural challenge.

First we had to get there. We pulled up anchor and left San Diego.

We sailed the entire distance of 1,000 miles over the next two weeks, only using the motor for about five hours, just long enough to charge batteries and fill up the water tanks. We arrived in Puerto Vallarta with a full tank of fuel.

We experienced rolly seas all the way to Cedros Island and Turtle Bay and the winds were steady, getting up to 30 knots. We sailed about 150 miles per day averaging a distance of 70–80 miles offshore. Generally it was warm weather but we got a lot of spray into the cockpit so we got wet and cold. We should have worn our foul weather gear.

When we got closer to shore, boat traffic and commercial traffic increased significantly. We talked to one freighter on the VHF and the crew was very helpful to us. The radio operator told us he saw us on his radar at eight miles and warned us of other freighter traffic coming. We promptly got away from the freighter track.

When we got closer to Santa Maria we saw a number of small fishing boats. What a relief to put down the anchor in the shallow waters at Santa Maria on a warm and quiet moonlit night. We had sailed steadily for four straight days and nights. For me as a non-sailor, that was a hugely significant accomplishment. And we did it with our three children. What a joy to share this kind of experience with them. They were wonderfully well-behaved and cooperative with us and with one another.

Santa Maria is a beautiful, quiet, wild, huge, shallow protected bay. It is easy to anchor in. We were exhausted after the trip and stayed put for two windy days at anchor. It was not very rolly and we were quite comfortable. Many cruising boats came and went.

We tried to get ashore but the surf was too high. So, we stayed on our boat and it was a great place for us to rest. Allan had a chance to fix more things—running lights, check the engine, and do laundry which dried fast in the wind and sun. With watermaker water, the boat got rinsed off, even our sails. On the second day Allan worked hard on our charts to get them organized with latitude and longitude waypoints put in to our handheld GPS. I spent a lot of time going through cupboards, provisions, cleaning the fridge, and cooking food.

We left for Cabo San Lucas at 07:30 on Sunday November 21, exactly one week after leaving San Diego. It was quite rolly at first and the swells ran high. It got really windy when we approached Cabo and a strong breeze came off the land. We were on a beam reach sail for the first time on this journey with a steady 25 knots of wind. The swells got smaller as we closed into shore and to the point. We arrived at Cabo with three other sailboats who were all on the same course.

We were really tired so Allan wisely suggested we stay at Cabo and anchor off the beach. We had no intention of going ashore because the marina and check-in were grossly expensive but we were glad to put down the hook (anchor) for 24 hours.

Looking back at our trip down the Baja, we were glad to have done that long leg quickly. The challenge was staying rested. The children seemed to quickly succumb to seasickness and we were going through a lot of Gravol. Seasickness is a troublesome thing and can be debilitating. Allan would work hard on setting the sails and navigating so that he tended to exhaustion and seasickness as well.

Joshua's comment about this stretch was, "Mom and Dad, off-shore sailing is like being on a roller coaster 24/7. And you can't get off." That certainly summed it up. And it was the "you can't get off" part that I did not like.

A highlight for Joshua on the trip was catching two tuna. We trailed a line behind our boat while underway and caught the fish. The first time it was a mess. The wind was picking up, swells were large and the boat was rolling. The fish was pulled on board, flapping and flipping. A large wave heaved the boat. Then there was blood, water and mess everywhere with Allan landing in the bucket sitting with the fish, narrowly missing the large cleaning knife flying across the cockpit with him. The second fish was a much smoother and calmer event. No mess. No fuss.

The single sideband radio was our lifeline during this leg. From this point on it became one of the most important pieces of equipment on board. We had set up a check-in time every morning with Dave Dobson, a Canadian cruiser who was still in San Diego. We called it the Canadian Baja Net, that eventually became the Amigo Net. It was wonderful to hear Dave's cheerful, positive, encouraging voice each day. As our trip progressed, more and more people joined in and participated on the net.

At Cabo we had a somewhat rolly, noisy place to stop. There were a few sailboats at anchor off the beach and we all rocked and rolled together. During the day the whole area was busy with ski-doos, fishing boats, big hotel amusements (parasailers, whale-watching trips). This spot was the famous beach where so many boats were lost during an unusual southerly storm called Hurricane Paul in 1982. It felt a bit unnerving to be parked in the same place as that tragedy.

One very unusual event that happened on our trip down the Baja occurred on our way out of Santa Maria when I was on watch. We had some difficulty with the engine and Allan had to work on it in rolly conditions for about an hour or two. He ended up exhausted and had to rest. I took the watch and chose to lay down for ten minute intervals in the cockpit. I set our alarm clock to go off every ten minutes, so that I would wake up if I fell asleep. Exhausted, I fell fast asleep and inadvertently slept for an hour! So much could have happened during that hour. Jumping awake, I bolted upright and looked around the horizon. I gasped at what was behind us. Two very large objects were behind our boat, and we had motored right between them. I suspect they were boats of some sort. The fact that our boat went between these two objects and they were not very far apart, while I was asleep, suggests to me that an angel was probably steering or at least on watch for us. To think we could have had a collision while I was on watch was a sickening thought.

At this point, thankful prayer was a constant practise in my heart. I felt a Divine Hand guiding and protecting us all the time. This situation put the spiritual in perspective for me once again. I do not know how it is possible for people to cope with crises in their lives without faith. Faith meant we could make this trip. Without faith, I could have never done it. Not with three children on board and me being a non-sailor. We did not meet many other boats with children on board during the entire trip.

JOSHUA'S JOURNAL

We are finally leaving San Diego. After two months of sitting in a marina I am sure the moss is thick under our keel.

I woke up early in the morning on Sunday, November 14 when the reality of leaving donned on me. We had breakfast and all of our friends came by in their dinghies and said good bye. We spent the rest of the morning making our ship sea worthy. In the afternoon we left. But first we had to get diesel and water at the fuel dock. We then left San Diego.

Out in the ocean it wasn't very rolly. As soon as he could Dad pulled out the sails. The wind was great and we clicked along at a good seven knots. The sun was out and it made for a good afternoon sail. By nightfall we were opposite the Coronado Islands. We kept making good headway with only 300 more miles to go. Thus ended our afternoon at sea. I might note that I took the evening watch until 22:00 hours. I wasn't very sick either.

Day 2: Everyone had good rest last night. I had the morning watch. It was a beautiful day and the swell wasn't that high. As I looked around, there was not a boat in sight. We had most of our sails out and there was a smashing breeze. It was warm too. We had breakfast and spent the morning resting. After lunch I hung our fishing line over the side of the boat. The swells were big and there was twenty five knots of wind. In half an hour we pulled in a small tuna. It was quite a battle to get the wriggling fish into the cockpit. But we did it. After bleeding the fish Dad started cutting it up. As he did so, a large wave rolled the boat and Dad, the fish and bucket of blood all fell and landed in a corner of the cockpit. It wasn't pleasant and was most uncomfortable for Dad. The fish did make a delicious dinner though. Later in the evening there was a lot freighter traffic. We talked to one on the VHF radio. That was neat.

Day 3: This morning we were opposite Isla Cedros, an island just north of Bahia Tortugas (Turtle Bay). We were about 60 miles off shore. Today, Dad got the wind vane steering system working. It is very accurate and powerful. It steers far better than you could by hand. Nothing happened to be made note of. We did not see many ships and I rested in the afternoon.

One thing that I don't like about the big choppy swell is getting seasick. I love the sailing and the fact that I don't have to do schoolwork en route.

Day 4: We have now been sailing for three days. It was time to start the engine because the batteries were down and needed charging up. When we started it, no water was going through the cooling system. Dad was able to fix it. He also started the water-maker and now we had lots of clear sparkling water to drink. In the evening we checked in and gave our weather on the Southbound Net at 19:00 hours. We were the only ones travelling down the Baja coastline.

Day 5: Each morning we talk to our friends the Dobson's on the SSB radio at 09:00 hours. They are from Vancouver, too. Today when I told them I hand steered the boat to 11.7 knots (about 17 km/hr) down a wave Mr. Dave declared me the Baja Surf King. It is very warm out and hot in the sun. I played Chinese checkers with Dad while the auto pilot steered the boat up to 11.8 knots (we never told Mr. Dave about that). By late afternoon we were only twenty miles from Bahia Santa Maria. I soon shouted "Land Ho." The land is very barren with few trees and lots of scrub. At nightfall mom and I had to go up on the deck in the cool wind look out for lobster traps. We dropped anchor at 19:30 hours in complete darkness. It was very warm and felt almost exactly like being in Hawaii. It was good to not be moving any more. This ended the longest time I have travelled non-stop and not touched land.

JOANNA'S JOURNAL

I am glad when we departed from San Diego. Then Monday came. We were 80 miles from any land and you couldn't see nothing but blue sky and blue water. When I say blue water I mean blue, blue water. It was rolly, really rolly and Joshua and Dad decided at the very worst moment to try fishing. Of course we caught a fish, a small tuna. Dad bled it and everything in the bucket and then a big wave came and he ended up sitting in the bucket! Still it was delicious! We had such a nice wind. And we had that for four days without stopping. On Tuesday we got the wind vane going and enjoyed the warm, warm sun. Oh that water was so pretty. On Thursday nearing the end of the day we shouted "Land Ho!" Me, Dad and Lydia sat on the deck and baked in the sun. Lydia and I played fun games in the front V berth for most of the trip.

JOANNA'S JOURNAL:

The Vast Wide Ocean
I could only see the blue blue waters,
The sun shone brightly down,
We were miles and miles from any town,
I felt alone at sea.
The dolphins were entertaining me,
The fish swam by,
The white fluffy clouds in the blue blue sky,
I was not alone at all.

I could see only the pink horizon,
the sun was going away,
I saw the last glimpse of the day,
Not a boat was in sight,
The moon and the stars shone so bright,
The sky was black,
A shooting star shot across the sky and back
I was not alone at all on the vast wide ocean.

The Autopilot
It's all full of levers and springs,
It's one of the neatest things.
It's a wonderful invention,
A machine not to mention.
Steering faithfully ahead,
We can sleep in our bed.
Stay to your course for hours on end,
Steering on straight without a bend.

LYDIA'S JOURNAL:

This is a summery (sic) of the last four days at sea. In the morning it was
blue sky and we were ROLLING!! We put out the fishing line and caught
a tuna about 10 or12 pounds. We bled it and while Dad was cutting it up

a big wave came and tossed him into the bucket where the fish was in. We had to clean out the cockpit which was really hard in the waves but it served a good dinner. I think tuna is my favourite fish now that I have tasted it. The next day we got the wind vane going. On Wednesday the engine didn't have water going through it. We fixed it quickly though. On Thursday we got to Santa Maria. The swells calmed down and it was hot and we went up on deck. We arrived at 7:30 pm and anchored. CALM AT LAST.

Oh, I've got a riddle for you: How do you find a 7-11 80 miles offshore? The answer is: surfing down a face of a wave. You either go 7 knots or 11 knots!

Lydia is referring here to the constant boat speed for many hours at a time of going from 7 knots in the trough of a wave to 11 knots surfing down the wave's face.

Never in my life before have I experienced such beauty, and fear at the same time.

—*Ellen MacArthur*

CHAPTER 21

The Crossing

We left Cabo by noon on Tuesday, November 23 to cross the Sea of Cortez. Our destination was Isla Isabella, an isolated bird sanctuary island made famous by French explorer Jacques Cousteau. It was a two-day trip and our toughest one yet.

It began with engine problems we had been having since leaving Bahia Magdalena. We could see that water was not coming out the stern vent, which meant the engine was not getting the cooling water. Allan replaced a small rubber seal and lubricated it well. That helped initially. A fellow cruiser suggested Allan check the impeller again even though it was a new one. We found that it was already broken again. After replacing the impeller, a seemingly small and insignificant rubber part, our coolant system began to work again.

When we left Cabo, however, we had another fright as the engine began to really overheat. After an hour or so Allan figured out that we were demanding too much power combined with the warm sea temperature (85°F or more) as the batteries were charging, the watermaker was pouring out fresh water, and the engine was pushing the boat along at a good speed. There was too much going on all at once. Once we slowed everything down, there was no problem. We got our batteries charged up, the water tanks full, the engine cooled down, and then the wind picked up.

We had two straight days of sailing. It was quiet and peaceful. Motoring in contrast is noisy, smelly and often goes along with unpleasant windless conditions. *Morning* is designed to sail really well in ocean conditions and she sailed beautifully crossing the Sea of Cortez. She is streamlined and strong, effortlessly skimming through the sea.

The first night across the Sea of Cortez, the wind was a steady 25 knots northwest. It finally became a close reach (close-hauled at first). The waves were huge; 15 feet high and exceptionally steep as they clashed against the tidal current. Allan felt these were the largest and most difficult seas we had been in yet. Riding along the crests of the tall pyramid shaped waves, he could not believe his eyes when he looked down and did not see any water under the boat on either side! It gave the appearance of being suspended in mid-air. Or had our boat suddenly taken flight? Undaunted, *Morning* handled the conditions perfectly.

Allan had to work very hard on the sail plan and ended up going on deck to attach the staysail. This was a difficult manoeuvre for him, and it took a long time to accomplish. The rolling of the boat was quick and vigorous. We got slammed by some very large waves.

The first 24 hours were horrendous. The wind was strong and the waves had built up to great heights. We were experiencing 700 miles of "fetch," a section of ocean surface over which the wind blows in a constant direction, thus generating the waves that were coming down the entire length of the Sea of Cortez. The wind was funneling down the Sea creating these unusually large steep waves. This was unrelenting for 12 hours while we sailed the first night away from Cabo. I had a late night watch and the conditions were wild. Somehow in the midst of being surrounded by all of nature's fury, I had a wonderful calmness and peace in my heart. The Bible calls it the peace that passes understanding. I knew we were right where we were supposed to be. I had an overwhelming sense of God's presence with us. Even if the unimaginable happened, and we perished, I was not troubled. I had such assurance and confidence even in the face of possible disaster. This was a "faith empowering" moment for me.

At that point, my faith was put to the test. And faith will be tested. I came to know faith is tangible, that faith is meaningful, and that faith works.

I heard it coming. I couldn't see it, but I could hear the mighty rush of water coming towards us.

Rogue waves rarely occur, and I do not know many people who have experienced them. But a giant rogue wave was now bearing down upon us, and I was sitting totally helpless in our cockpit. Time stood still to me as I waited for it to crash on top of *Morning*.

Rushing, gushing, raging waters hurled themselves at our boat. I held my breath. It hit. Hard.

Morning and I went under the avalanche of water for a few seconds. Surprisingly, the water was very warm and the boat bobbed quickly to the top of the waves. I was in shock but immediately grateful for the good cockpit drains, for a harness securing me to the boat, for water tight hatches (no water entered inside the boat where the family was sleeping), and for such a capable boat.

What an experience; one I would never forget.

The whole family was fast asleep down below and had no idea what had happened. Only Joanna woke up, and called out to me to make sure I was all right. I assured her that all was well and she went back to sleep.

The second day of travel was sublime. The seas had settled and the wind was down to an idyllic 15 knots. We were on a broad reach with a low ocean swell. Allan stayed in bed all day. He felt quite sick, queasy, and was exhausted. The long trip from San Diego caught up to him all at once. We finally had perfect sailing conditions and he was able to relax and sleep. By evening he perked right up and took a long watch so that I could sleep. And did I sleep!

We were entertained on this leg of travel. A group of dolphins accompanied our boat for at least an hour. Our children were harnessed to the boat and made their way to the bow. They shouted, clapped, and cheered the frolicking mammals along. The dolphins seemed to hear and responded with bigger leaps, splashes, and gymnastics. Later, at dusk, a large bird decided to sit on our bow. Content to have a ride for a few hours, we got lots of photos of our feathered visitor who was oblivious to our presence.

We arrived at Isla Isabella by 09:00. We were so thankful that we could find that tiny island in the Sea of Cortez by plotting our course using our compass and GPS and taking our latitude and longitude positions. At that time, its position on the available charts was not shown correctly. Somehow I wondered if it would work. Our confidence increased as we successfully made landfall.

Isla Isabella is an impressive-looking island. It has an amazing number of birds constantly flying above it. It is rugged, spectacular, and isolated. It has colourful red volcanic cliffs lined with lush green tropical scrub. However, it has an inhospitable coastline lined with pounding surf.

We came into the anchorage—a questionable spot, in my mind—and there was one other sailboat. It was a challenge to anchor in rolly conditions. We had to avoid a huge rock that was somewhere in the bay and we never did anchor properly. The anchor just kind of lay on the bottom amidst all the rocks. Some cruisers had nicknamed the anchorage the "anchor-eater."

We had hoped to get ashore but we did not even attempt it. Allan was not comfortable with the idea of us leaving the boat. We did jump in for a swim, however, and the water was delightfully warm. Rinse off was easy with our freshwater hose in the cockpit.

By Friday morning, November 26, we were on our way for a six-hour run to San Blas, Menatchen Bay. It was a motoring day. The air was very warm. We sat together in the cockpit reading.

We put down the hook in expansive Menatchen Bay. At that moment a huge fish cuddled next to our hull. It was a whale shark more than half the length of our boat, and for some unknown reason decided to hang out beside us. Not really a pleasant experience, although the children were quite delighted looking at its long brown spotted back. I thought it was big and ugly, and didn't really want to look at it closely. Some marine life I prefer to look at from a distance. No one was inclined to jump in the water for a swim.

We found the area had a lot of bugs but it was a wonderfully quiet, peaceful, calm night. What a difference it made to everyone's dispositions the next morning to have a good sleep.

The next morning we were underway early, motoring towards the little seaside town of Chacala. En route atop glassy seas we had the watermaker running and Allan and Joshua were doing our laundry in the cockpit. They used a Rubbermaid container and the toilet plunger. We were getting pretty resourceful while underway and we had a lot of laundry by this time.

It was a time for reflection. I was thankful that we had traveled over 3,000 miles to Mexico. My prayer was that our time in Mexico would be a time to rest, relax, get strong, and stay healthy. It had been an extraordinary amount of effort and concentration to get to this part of Mexico. I prayed for Allan. His diligence in fixing, replacing and maintaining the boat was tremendous. He was doing what none of us could do. Alone, Allan carried a huge load of responsibility. So far, he had taken good care of his family and had made wise decisions.

I was starting to realize the risk we were taking on this trip. I prayed God would protect us.

LYDIA'S JOURNAL

Today we left to head across the Sea of Cortez! There was no wind and not much swell. Further out we stopped our engine and sailed. The swells were growing HUGE. In the evening it went up to 25 knots of wind so we put up the stay sail. That night waves came crashing over our boat. Roaring, rushing, the mounds of water either passed over on top of us or underneath us. Some waves filled up the cockpit with water. Dad said these were the highest, steepest and fastest waves he had ever seen! The next day it was lovely. In the morning the waves were still high. They got calmer and the wind died down.

In the morning we rested, played games and kept watch. In the afternoon dolphins came over to us and played in the bow wake it was so neat! We talked with them and sang and clapped our hands. They jumped and spun in the air. Even Sea World couldn't beat that! They made noises and stayed a long time. It was a great show! That night there was only 10 knots of wind. We were going 6 knots with a gyb, staysail and mainsail! That night was not as exciting as our first. One more story and then it's time for bed! After the dolphins left, over came a bird with fur all around his neck, eyes, and beak. The rest of him was all feathers. We sat at the bow of our boat and he sat one foot away from us. He was pretty tame. We got some good pictures of him on our camera. He stayed with us all night! I guess he hadn't been near people for his whole entire life.

JOANNA'S JOURNAL

I'm rather far behind again because of this travelling business. Today is the 27th and we haven't set foot on land for two weeks! Anyways, we left Cabo, which was hot, dry with warm water of 85 degrees F. by the way! The first day of crossing the Sea of Cortez was awful! It was bumpy and lumpy! But by the 2nd day was bright, sunny and warm. Dolphins came and put on an hour long show! Then a bird which had been following us since Cabo came and took a ride on our pulpit. He was really cute and so we took lots of pictures! On the third day we caught the most beautiful fish, a Mahi Mahi, it got away, too bad.

A tourist remains an outsider throughout his visit; but a
sailor is part of the local scene from the moment he arrives.
—*Anne Davison*

CHAPTER 22

Mexican Immersion

Anchoring off of the village of Chacala for over one week and acclimatizing
to the Mexican mainland was a wonderful break and the beginning of our
Mexican immersion experience. We put out a bow anchor and stern anchor
so that we faced into the swell and never broadside to it. We loved this
anchorage but very few sailboats lingered here because they did not use both
a bow and stern anchor. Consequently they sat broadside to the seas and
rolled from gunnel to gunnel. Miserable. So, they left. Which meant we had
the bay to ourselves for most of our time at Chacala.

In San Diego, we had met a cruiser named Phil who lived on a catamaran
called *Manna Sea*. He loved cruising the Mexican mainland coastline and
recommended Chacala as his favourite stopover. He convinced us that it was
well worth the visit, so we planned for it. As a result we had a wonderful
introduction to Mexico. This small rural vacation spot was ideal for us to
enter and experience Mexican culture. Urban Mexicans love Chacala and
visit the area in droves, especially during holidays and Easter.

We loved poking around and exploring the village. Hiking the small
nearby volcano crater gave us a great view of Chacala and the soon-to-be-
developed beach around the corner. In the town we met a variety of people.
By visiting the schools four times, once to the one-room secondary school
and three times to the elementary school, our children had the opportunity
to meet and enjoy the local children. We were warmly received and had a
lot of fun especially in the elementary school. We presented each child with
a pencil and a paper snowflake that our children made. We brought a small
Canadian flag and sang "O Canada" to the class. The primary class sang

the Mexican anthem back to us and in orderly proper fashion stood up to receive us when we entered the classroom and sat down when we left. We gave the teachers Canadian pencils, flag pins, postcards, and origami birds that our children had made.

With the Grade 4, 5, and 6 classes we had 45 minutes with them in the Bibliotec (library). We showed them how to cut out paper snowflakes. Joanna demonstrated how to make a stork in origami. All of the students were thrilled. It was such simple and wholesome fun. Outside on the gravel field, Joshua enjoyed playing soccer with the boys. It was a delight for our children to share with and enjoy the Mexican children, who were the same age.

The library or Bibliotec was built by Rotary International and was being run by Susanna Escobido, an American, who lived in Chacala for four months in the winter. She had done a marvellous job and encouraged us to return and assist in any programs that we could. She gave us a tour of the town, up and down the side streets and past the backyards. Red dirt, strong aromatic smells, crowing roosters, loud mariachi music blaring, burning garbage... this was Mexico, in a typical Mexican village.

Triny gave us Spanish lessons in her home. Through her we met relatives and friends especially at the homes of her mother-in law, Loupe and friend, Guadaloupe. These two women made fresh tortillas daily and we made our orders. The fresh homemade tortillas were scrumptious. They were a welcomed change from the canned food we had been eating.

Fresh food was available at the local tienda (store) and there were fruit and vegetables from the vegetable man, who came by in his truck every other day. Fresh whole chicken, fresh eggs, tortillas, limes, avocados, tomatoes, and oranges were always available. From the vegetable man, we could buy huge papayas as well as fresh chilies, peppers, and limes. It was wonderful to have easy access to all this fresh delicious food. Our daily menus changed radically.

We loved buying fresh fish. I called it the ultimate "fast food" because it is so quick and easy to pan fry.

We tried out a couple of the local palapas (small restaurants on the beach). A full dinner cost $40 Canadian for the five of us. We felt it was a little risky to eat the locally prepared food too frequently. Most of our cruising friends got ill during the cruising season in Mexico. With three children on board, I was determined to keep the family from getting sick. Before leaving home I had purchased bottles of nutribiotic drops that we took before and after every meal that we had on shore. Nutribiotic is made from grapefruit seed extract, a highly concentrated and remarkably effective form of citric acid, and a mainstay for us throughout the cruising season. It's one of the main reasons that our family stayed healthy for the entire year that we were away.

Our children loved the swimming at Chacala bay. They swam off the beach, in the surf, or around our boat while visiting all the other boats. Local boys from Chacala would come and swim around the cruising boats as well. This is how we met two brothers, Carlos and Alfredo. They came out regularly and Joshua loved to go off swimming with them. He was able to understand their Spanish and he taught them some English. On our last evening in Chacala we had some time with Carlos and Alfredo to read some simple Spanish and English to them. They loved it and happily joined in for half an hour.

LYDIA'S JOURNAL

Chacala is a small resort village for Mexicans. It has a few Palapas (Mexican restaurants) lining the beach, two small tiendas (stores) and a couple of houses. There is also a church and a school. We love this place and recommend it to everybody. We walked the golden sand beaches. We saw magnificent views from an overgrown volcano when we hiked way up in the jungle. Hot weather will welcome you and warm swimming water. Watch out for rays and jellyfish though. Green palm trees and shrubby bushes line the hillside. We all loved visiting the school. We made paper snowflakes with the children, sang O Canada, gave them pencils and they sang to us and included us in their activities. We all had a lot of fun. Chacala is a lovely spot with few people. You all would enjoy it.

JOANNA'S JOURNAL

At 7 am we were on our way to the Secondary School. We spent about
30 minutes there giving pencils, postcards, showing pictures and so on.
The class had 15 people in it and the room was down to bare bones.
Dirt floor, a few chairs scattered, no door and no glass in the windows.
The primary school was a lot nicer, it had 20 people. The one class sang
happy birthday to 14 year old Joshua. We had great fun.

But Jesus said, Suffer little children, and forbid them not, to come unto me: for of such is the kingdom of heaven. Matthew 19:14

CHAPTER 23

An Orphanage

My parents visited us every three or four months while we were on our trip. Their visits were a highlight and gave us something to look forward to. They met us in Puerto Vallarta and we had a wonderful week with them. We stayed with them in a large spacious condominium that they rented. It was amazing to sleep on land, in a real bed. Luxury! We deeply appreciated these times of respite off the boat.

The highlight of our week in this popular tourist town was our afternoon at Casa Hogar, an orphanage for 52 children cared for by four Catholic nuns. What a wonderful time we had there. The cruising community organized a Christmas evening for the orphans. We heard about it and were invited to attend. Joshua, Joanna, and Lydia happily played with the children. Joshua played soccer with the boys. Joanna and Lydia were skipping, running around and holding hands with the little girls. When the other cruisers arrived, we sang Christmas songs together. There were piñatas, dinner, then gift giving. We helped as we could. I enjoyed scooping up some of the little children and cuddling them. One little girl wouldn't finish her dinner, so I picked her up and she happily let me spoon-feed her. Another little cherub-faced laughing boy wanted to be picked up too, so I finally did. I cuddled and rocked him and he fell fast asleep in my arms.

When we left the orphanage, the children enthusiastically waved to us. My mom had also done her share of holding and cuddling a lot of children. It was a marvellous time for all of us. This was a chance for our family to share and to give. This was living at its best. Our hearts were expressed and received.

JOSHUA'S JOURNAL

All over Latin America during the month of December, little folk operas called posadas take place in small towns and in the large cities. For the ten days before Christmas these posadas are staged. The posada is a re-enactment of Joseph and Mary's arrival in Bethlehem and their search for a room. In small towns, groups of people walk around the neighbourhood singing at the doors of people's houses. It is sung in Spanish, of course.

The cruisers in Puerto Vallarta give support to an orphanage in the outskirts of the city where some of them help organize a posada for the children there. We were all invited to come on the evening of December fifteenth. When my family and I arrived we were greeted by one of the nuns and a throng of children. Inside, it was quite large with two courtyards and eight dormitories. There are four nuns to take care of fifty-two children. We were the first people to arrive so I spent my time getting acquainted with the boys. They were very friendly and I was able to talk to them with the Spanish that I had learned. I played soccer with them until the posada started.

The posada started and this is what we did. Half of the cruisers and children went inside in to the dormitories. The other half stayed outside. On the outside was the group with Joseph and Mary. They started singing, asking for a room and a bed for the tired Mary. The inside group was the inn keeper and replied that his inn was full. The outside group then moved on to the next door and the scene was repeated. The song ended by Joseph finally being invited in and blessing the inn keeper. The next activity was the cracking open of piñatas. Each child was blindfolded and given a turn at swinging a stick. I helped some of the boys on the roof pull on the rope attached to the piñata. The piñatas were filled with candy, nuts, and fruit. It was great to see the children enjoying themselves.
Some of the cruising families helped serve a dinner that was typically Mexican. We had pozole soup which is a chicken broth with cabbage, radishes and Mexican corn. The corn is called mais. It is very coarse and

has to be chewed thoroughly. I thought it was quite good.

After the dinner, Santa Claus arrived. All the children were very excited. We walked to one of the dormitories where the presents were stacked neatly in a corner. Each child had to stand in line and wait his turn. Most of them were very surprised when they received a present. For some of the young children, it was their first present they'd ever been given. I enjoyed the Mexican Christmas very much. I hope to experience some more Mexican traditions while we are still in Mexico.

LYDIA'S JOURNAL

Gram and us went to the orphanage to a dinner and a play and sort of a party. It was really fun. Cruisers support this orphanage and help out.

I made one good friend. I don't know much Spanish so we used sign language and I said as much Spanish as I knew. Dad and Mom and Gram held lots of very wet babies. Dad even changed a really cute baby boy. We ran around lots and Santa Claus even came! (He was just a dressed up Cruiser of course). There were also some piñatas. When all the candy fell out all the orphans flocked and fell on it like a group of seagulls diving and fighting for dead fish!

JOANNA'S JOURNAL

I wish time wouldn't fly so fast! After Grandpa left for the airport, things began to get exciting- we went to a celebration at an orphanage. We had great fun meeting other children. We got to bed at 1:00 am in the morning that night!! Those children (I made a lot of friends) sure made me run around until I was wishing for my bed!

Bad cooking is responsible for more trouble at sea than all other things put together.

—*Thomas Fleming Day*

CHAPTER 24
Anchored

Leaving Puerto Vallarta Christmas Eve on an overnight sail south, we arrived in Tenacatita early on Christmas Day morning. It was a tiring overnight sail from Puerto Vallarta to Tenacatita. Arriving Christmas Day morning, we were somewhat unconventional in travelling on Christmas Eve. No other boats were out that night anywhere within the 1,000 miles or more that our radio would reach. Upon our arrival, we were immediately welcomed to Tenacatita by the unofficial mayor, Darrell, in a zodiac from his vessel *Black Swan*. Darrell and his wife Sandy anchored in Tenacatita and lived on their sailboat for two months of each year. Tenacatita was their favourite cruising spot on the Mexican coast. Every cruiser we spoke with said the same thing. As did our guidebooks. Tenacatita was also our favourite stop during our entire year of travel. We had a total of two idyllic months at anchor in Tenacatita Bay.

Darrell surprised us with a spontaneous invitation to a cruisers Christmas potluck dinner on *Capricorn Cat*, a large catamaran anchored in the centre of the bay. We were grateful for this thoughtful invitation. Frankly, we did not have much planned for Christmas Day. Allan and I were exhausted from the trip south and needed a day to recover. However, we all hugely enjoyed the wonderful dinner and meeting more cruisers as we spread out on the deck of the spacious catamaran.

JOANNA'S JOURNAL

This is what we did for Christmas: there are lots of boats in the bay including a large catamaran. So the cat invited all the cruisers for a pot luck. There was lots to eat! What a neat way to spend Christmas. It's kind of neat to be able to swim on Christmas!

JOSHUA'S JOURNAL

Today is Christmas. I am so happy! When I got up we were about 6 miles north of Tenacatita. We arrived around 10 am. It is a very large bay with a lot of sailboats in it. We anchored and a man from Black Swan came over in his dinghy and invited us for a potluck dinner at the only catamaran in the bay. It is called Capricorn Cat.

Meanwhile, Mom made pancakes for breakfast. We gave our presents to each other. I gave Dad a book of his favourite poet's writings that I bought in San Diego. He was very pleased. After all our hard work we had to rest. Mom then let us swim off the boat. Imagine swimming in the winter and especially on Christmas Day!! The water was very warm.

We felt we had arrived home. In a sense we had reached our ultimate destination for the year. We did travel for a few weeks a little further south, but basically Tenacatita was where we anchored and stayed put. We lived in t-shirts, shorts and bathing suits all of the time. We had perfect weather every day in this large protected and spacious anchorage. No bugs, not too humid, comfortable, and lots to do.

We were impressed by the camaraderie and helpfulness of the cruisers in the anchorage. Fifteen to forty boats anchored in Tenacatita at any one time. Tenacatita is a huge protected bay bordered by a three-mile-long sandy beach. It is considered the safest and most pleasant anchorage on the Mexican mainland west coast.

Every Friday night there was a dinghy raft-up get-together for the cruisers in the middle of the bay. It was a great way to meet other cruisers. Our children were fascinated by all the interesting characters we met from different boats. For example, Joshua loved meeting the ex-marine Navy Seals who had incredible life experiences to share.

We loved Tenacatita Bay. The little town of La Manzanilla is three miles across the bay. Once a week we took our sailboat across the bay to provision, charge up the batteries, and run our watermaker. We bought fresh hot tortillas from the tortilleria, freshly-caught fish at the fish market, and an abundance of fresh fruit and vegetables. At a little tienda we ordered chicken one morning. We were asked if we could wait for half an hour. In 30 minutes we received our chicken that was still warm (just butchered). You could say it was as fresh as you could get. We also visited the butcher where they had beef and pork available. It was also fresh and warm that morning. Without refrigeration, shopping happened early and by 10:00 or 11:00 there was not much of anything left.

We developed an easy routine in Tenacatita starting with an early breakfast while taking part in the Amigo Net, the informal radio net on single sideband radio that began in San Diego by a few of us Canadian boats travelling south to Mexico. It was on 8.122 khz on upper single sideband at 08:00 Puerto Vallarta time.

After breakfast we went ashore for the morning. Our inflatable dinghy with a 5 horsepower motor was lowered into the water. We painstakingly motored to shore through the surf and reefs that framed the anchorage. On shore, we dragged our dinghy high up on the sand, then walked a mile along the beach to one end where we swam and body-surfed for a few hours in the 78°F water. It was a leisurely relaxed walk back to our dinghy while we collected unusual shells. The antics of pelicans and snowy egrets entertained us.

Back to our dinghy, which was parked above the high water mark at the other end of the beach, we dragged it into the water. Carefully timing our departure through the surf was challenging in the constant changing tidal conditions. Then it was lunchtime on the boat. Followed by the Mexican siesta; two hours on our berths reading during the hottest time of the day. In the afternoon it was swim time off the boat. Allan roped up a long plank in the rigging to act as a diving board, which the children loved jumping off.

JOANNA'S JOURNAL

In the morning we had the funnest time playing, swimming and walking on the beach. A lot of people are afraid of waves (the big ones) but I'm not a bit afraid of them, so it's tons of fun!

Since we had the three dinghies, the children could all get off the boat to sail, motor or row. If it was breezy in the afternoon, the children, especially Joshua, loved to rig up our dinghy and sail around the anchorage greeting all the cruisers on their anchored boats. It was here in Tenacatita that each of our three children learned to confidently sail solo. It was with real delight that Allan and I watched Lydia get to the point where she headed off on her own.

We always ate an early dinner. Frequently we would invite other cruisers over to our boat for a potluck dinner. These occasions became more and more regular as we got to know more folks.

Because there was so much to do in Tenacatita with swimming, snorkeling, dinghy sailing, boogie boarding, walking beaches, shell collecting, and bird watching, we did not do much boat maintenance or a lot of schoolwork. For example, one of our favourite day excursions was motoring up the three mile long lagoon in our inflatable boat. It is called "the jungle ride" because of the lush mangrove that forms thick walls and a canopy over the long narrow winding waterway. We did this excursion a number of times. One time we enjoyed a day with Paula and Vlad from the boat Tethys. They "borrowed" our children for the ride up and took a real interest in instructing our children in the types and habitats of the birds and fish we encountered. On that occasion we saw a mother opossum with five little babies, an iguana, a raccoon, and alligators. It was a gorgeous trip.

The jungle ride was so popular with our children, that our Joanna wrote a novel called *The Mangrove Secret*. The romance of it all had a profound effect on her sensitive creative imagination.

JOANNA'S JOURNAL

I decided today I would write a novel called "The Mangrove Secret." I've just started planning it. It will take place in the Mangrove by the river!

JOSHUA'S JOURNAL

Our family woke up very early and we had an early start. Dad wanted to go early on the jungle trip so we could see the birds before they were scared off by others. It was three miles up a winding, twisting river. In some places the bushes grow over the river and form a tunnel. At the end it opens right up and comes in behind the first bay that we saw when we first approached Bahia Tenacatita. The ride back was great!

At the far end of the jungle ride there is a fabulous snorkeling hole in the outer bay of Tenacatita called the aquarium. Our family, outfitted in wetsuits, would spend a couple of hours in the crystal clear water. Huge schools of small fish swarmed around us as we swam. We took turns holding our breath and swimming down as deep as we could. The aquarium was filled with an incredible variety of tropical fish. Our children were a little startled to see large moray eels poking out of crevices only a few feet away.

Our tentative Lydia transformed into a fearless swimmer and snorkeler at the aquarium. She loved gently hanging on to her dad while they paddled together on the water surface. Then, before I knew it, she had cleared her snorkel and was diving down deep into the water next to her father. It was the most beautiful thing to watch. Lydia became braver and braver, loving her new found freedom, and the adventure of it all.

Joshua and Joanna paired off, swimming, holding their breath, diving deep. They greatly increased in their power and endurance, as they probed and examined nooks, crannies, rocky ledges, and the sandy ocean floor. I only glanced at them from time to time, since they were completely engaged in their explorations.

Another highlight in Tenacatita was the wonderful Christmas/New Year's celebration put on by the cruisers for the poorest children in the local neighbourhood area. There was food and fun. But most of all, every child was given a large gift bag. It contained a soccer ball, toothbrush, toothpaste, notebook, pencils, and loads of candy. Our children had one delightful afternoon bagging 120 bags of candy for these little children and had the privilege of helping to hand out the bags. The Mexican children were beautifully dressed for the event, which was held on shore at a local open air restaurant. It was well organized, well attended and it was wonderful to see the generosity and care of the cruisers. This was a meaningful experience for everyone involved.

Living on the water is a unique experience in itself. Since we were now getting closer to the equator, dusk was at 18:00 and dawn was abrupt at 06:00. At night it was really dark. No cities or towns were nearby, so there was no artificial light. The phosphorescence was astounding in this location. Our children simply needed to stir the water up with their fingers, and the water lit up. When we travelled at night in our dinghy, the wake was a shimmering highway behind us in the dark.

One morning we woke up to the sound of rain pounding on the water. Well, at least it sounded like rain. Since we hadn't experienced rain for months, we looked outside and saw literally thousands of little fish jumping up and down out of the water everywhere. Startling, but wonderful.

At the end of our two months in Tenacatita there were almost forty boats in the anchorage. And we knew most of them. A giant pig roast was held on the beach to celebrate the birthdays of many of the cruisers, including Darrell, our unofficial mayor. For five hours, all the cruisers congregated on the beach at a local palapa. A pig was roasted on an open spit, and tables were set up for a huge potluck buffet. It was an amazing time together. One of the cruisers named Eric from *Makai* gave all the children surfing lessons. The children had a wonderful time, surfing together. Joshua and Joanna borrowed his surf board and actually stood up in the waves. Lydia played in the lagoon area making sandcastles with a group of girls. Our children played, swam and surfed for hours. They were completely exhausted by the end of the day, but it had been wonderful fun and an organizational feat by the crew of three of the boats in the anchorage.

LYDIA'S JOURNAL

In Tenacatita there are two large bays. We anchored our sailboat in the most protected bay where there is a long lagoon. You can take your dinghy up to the very end of the lagoon which is about 3 miles long. One day we set out in our dinghy to go up the lagoon. It is long and windy like a river. It is green, lush, humid and jungle-like. Outside of the lagoon in the bay where we have anchored, it is dry with cactus the size of trees. About half the trip the thick mangrove bushes form a roof over our heads and it is very, very narrow at times. There is only room for one dinghy to go up this lagoon. It took us almost an hour each way with a five horsepower motor and five people. Snowy egrets and other birds line the bushes on either side. A large iguana swam across our path. A mother opossum with her five babies walked across a branch over top of our heads. The lagoon ended at the first bay at its beach. We had a nice walk on the 2 mile long beach. The lagoon is deep and water is very murky. It is a great trip but watch out for pangas (Mexican boats) coming the other way.

A day in Tenacatita: In the morning we went to the beach for a walk and a swim. The waves were larger for body surfing so that was really fun. We came back to the boat to have lunch and rests. After that we got the sailing dinghy set up. We all went rowing, swimming and sailing , it was really fun. After that we had dinner.

New Year's Eve: In Tenacatita we had our regular routine for the day. Then in the evening we went to a floatation. Its when all the cruisers dinghies raft up and bring food and you pass it around. We brang [sic] lots of popcorn. We talked lots and watched the last sun for 1000 YEARS!! Then everybody went back to their boats to get their old flares to shoot them off for the New Year. They just about landed on our boat but didn't.

New Year's Day: We survived Y2K! The world is still existing. There was no problems at all in the world.

January 3, 2000: Today we did our regular routine of: breakfast, walk to the end of the beach, body surf there, walk back, lunch, read, boating, sailing/rowing and swimming, dinner. We also saw a turtle.

February: Today when we tried to get out of the surf we saw a gap through the waves so we went. We did it a little late and a huge wave loomed up ahead of us. We went over it half a second before it broke. We would have flipped backwards if we didn't have Mariah's children in the dinghy. We were SOAKED! We had the family from Mariah over for dinner. We played Monopoly.

JOANNA'S JOURNAL

January 3: This morning we had pancakes for about the fourth time in a row! Mom is reading "Pat of Silver Bush (by Lucy Maud Montgomery) and quoted "Pat wanted Silver Bush to be a place of food, love and rest." Mom said our boat should be like that too. Well, we're sure getting the food part! We had a great morning at the beach, then a good afternoon of boating!

January 4: We went boating and swimming in the afternoon. This cruising life is great!

JOSHUA'S JOURNAL

On waking up I read then got dressed for breakfast. I have not put on shoes for weeks!! We live in bathing suits!!

We did our usual walk on and swim at the beach. Every day here in Mexico it is sunny without a cloud in the sky!

I am now writing on January 1, 2000. I'm still here. I survived! Last night our family got ready to go to the dinghy raft up at 5 pm (just before dark at 6). Dad made heaps of popcorn which we brought. There was about

14 dinghies and they all had good food. We watched the sun set for the last time in 1000 years. Two hours later we headed back to the boat. The phosphorescence is spectacular! It glitters when you turn the outboard on! At midnight some of the cruiser's let off fireworks (their old flares actually!). It was neat to watch.

January 4: Today schoolwork ruled! We did not go to the beach but went to school (on our boat, that is)!! My Spanish is coming along fine. We had lunch, then a cruiser (from Campbell River) came over to our boat to help us sort our fishing gear. We got another tuna rig set up (our last one fell overboard when we were underway). After our rest, Lydia and I went sailing together. There was a good breeze and we sailed around the whole bay!

January 5: Today we did something different. We hauled up our anchor and headed across Tenacatita Bay to the little town of La Manzanilla. It is different from the other Mexican towns we have seen. The town is unfinished everywhere. We headed straight for a grocery store and bought a few necessities. Two healthy, organic chickens were butchered just for us. We bought some fish and meat steak. I thought the town was different and very, very poor. Getting off the beach was a little difficult. We went back and anchored in our exactly same spot that we left!

January 7: When we went body-surfing in front of the hotel I wore my flippers. I had a lot of fun surfing down the face of the wave. The water remains very warm for winter and the sun will give really bad burns to exposed skin during 11 am and 3 pm. That is the time we are not in it (we have lunch and rests then).

January 9: More of the same routine this morning. I don't think it will ever get boring!! One day blends into another! I had a lot of fun sailing our dinghy in the afternoon! I can visit everyone in the anchorage that way! And cruisers like to visit with me!

January 18: We are still in Tenacatita and today is laundry day! We turned our boat and the beach into a custom sized Laundromat!! In the morning Dad and I took all the dirty clothes to the beach. We used water from the palapa and did 18 trips back and forth with five gallon jugs. It was hard work, but then we earned our quesidillas at lunch time. After lunch and a rest we packed up the rocker stoppers (these really help our boat from rolling around too much in the swell) in preparation for leaving tomorrow for Melaque. I helped Dad put our dinghies away. It was a very busy day!

Difficulties are just things to overcome, after all.

—*Ernest Shackleton*

CHAPTER 25

Giant Manta Ray

The biggest adventure that took place on our trip occurred at Tenacatita Bay. Joshua wrote up the entire incident for *Latitude 38* magazine, which I have included at the end of this chapter. The experience changed all of us, but Joshua especially.

It was an ordinary sunny afternoon and we had finished our siestas. Lydia decided to swim off of the boat and the others were reading or laying on the boat deck. Lydia suddenly shot up our swim ladder to get out of the water. She was noticeably shaken up by something she had seen in the water. She thought it was a shark, but excitedly told us it was something very, very large. We did not know what to think about her story, since Lydia was not prone to exaggeration. But there was nothing for us to do, so we carried on with our afternoon plans.

We all needed to go ashore to get fresh water from the tap at the local palapa. We motored in and carried our water jugs up to the tap. It took a bit of time to fill our water jugs. While Allan and Joshua were returning to our boat with filled jugs, they noticed that one of the twenty boats in the anchorage was moving, with no one on it. It was *Neener 3*, a brand new 45-foot sailboat moving on its own, around the anchorage! The anchor rode was shaking and a couple of large fins broke the surface of the water. None of us could imagine what it was.

Allan and Joshua wasted no time at all. They jumped into our Avon, shot through the surf and zoomed up to *Neener 3*. Allan gave Joshua instructions and Joshua jumped aboard the transom, while the boat was moving at about four knots. Joshua grabbed the steering wheel and was able to steer the boat quickly away from *Halcyon*, a neighbouring boat. Providentially, the "thing" that was towing the boat also slightly turned away at the same time.

Finally Allan was able to see that it was a giant manta ray. It was 18 feet across. It had got itself tangled in *Neener 3's* chain rode and was pulling the boat around the anchorage on collision course with all the boats around it. We realized that it must have been the manta ray that had swum past Lydia earlier on. Unbelievable. Unimaginable. What a freaky phenomenon and what an amazing monstrous sea creature!

Allan quickly motored to *Neener 3*, attached our inflatable dinghy on to the transom, and climbed aboard to assist Joshua. Darryl arrived and got the engine started and the electric windlass going. They steered *Neener 3* away from the boats that were in the path of the fast-moving manta ray. Don, from *T Tauri Wind* and Tim, from *Treopia* arrived on the scene. Don assisted with pulling in the rode, while Tim free dove to the ocean bottom to try and get the chain rode off of the giant creature.

It was a little disconcerting sitting on the beach watching all the commotion. Fins were flipping frantically and a moving 30,000-pound sailboat like a battering ram running at sailboats in the anchorage. Tim was in the water, ducking up and down beside the sailboat and between Don in the dinghy then disappearing under everyone, taking big breaths before diving below again. More dinghies were arriving on the scene. Joanna, Lydia and I were sitting on the beach wondering what on earth was going on.

Finally Pete and Jean, the owners of *Neener 3* arrived back to their boat. They had spent the day going on the jungle mangrove ride. What a terrible shock for them to see a pile of people on their boat, and their boat in a completely different location from where they had anchored it.

Tim, the diver, did the miraculous and after many attempts, he unwrapped the anchor rode from the trapped animal. He free-dove 30 feet down to the manta ray that was resting on the ocean floor. Finally, the ray went free, floated to the surface with a flick of a large fin, then disappeared underwater.

What an amazing feat! The manta ray was freed, the sailboat didn't lose its rode and anchor, and no boats were damaged in the anchorage. In the entire process a whole group of people quickly worked in choreographed fashion and magically came together to work as an efficient capable team.

The owners of *Neener 3* were in shock. It took them days to recover from the incident. They were very upset by the whole ordeal even though their boat survived unscathed.

Once somewhat recovered, they organized a potluck raft-up a few days later at 17:00 around their boat. It was quite an experience to see twenty dinghies attached together, gently bobbing up and down in the low ocean swell as folks passed around plates of appetizers.

Darrell, the mayor, presented certificates of merit from the Tenacatita Cruisers' Association to thank Tim the diver and Joshua for their help. Joshua was asked to read out his written official account of what had happened. Joshua was presented with a Ray Rider t-shirt and presents from the owners of *Neener 3*. It was a memorable evening and brought all the cruisers in the anchorage together in a meaningful way. This was a story that quickly made its way up and down the coastline by radio. From this point on, wherever we went, Joshua was asked to share the story and his part in the action.

JOSHUA'S JOURNAL

We are in Bahia Tenacatita on the Mexican Gold Coast. In the anchorage here there are about twenty boats. This incident occurred in the afternoon of Saturday, January 15, 2000.

The afternoon was very warm and pleasant. Dad and I had just finished getting our water jugs filled and were on our way back from the beach to the boat. We were just passing a boat in the middle of the anchorage called "Neener 3" when we noticed something unusual. The anchor rode was moving back and forth very quickly. A large fin then appeared near Neener's anchor rode and the boat gave a sudden lurch to starboard. We called for the owners but no one was home. Dad motored over to the out-stretched anchor chain and we found ourselves over a very large sea animal, whatever it was. We realized that it was a lot larger than we had imagined. By this time the boat was careening around the middle of the anchorage with the safety of twenty boats at stake. Neener was now moving at a fast rate towards the nearest boat. I managed to jump off our dinghy onto the transom of Neener. I got to the wheel just in time to make a turn, avoiding a T-bone collision with "Halcyon". It was a close call and I was sweating hard.

Mr. Don from "Windward Luv" put a call out for help on the radio. Suddenly, dinghies arrived from everywhere. Mr. Darrell from "Black Swan" boarded Neener along with my Dad. They started the engine and manned the windlass. Neener started bearing down on Halcyon but for the second time I was able to steer the boat out of the way. The new arrivals in their dinghies were ready to act as fenders at a moment's notice. Mr. Tim from "Treopia" soon arrived and was madly fitting on his mask and fins. He was soon in the water wrestling to get to the anchor rode which was tangled around the sea animal. Mr. Don from "T Tauri Wind" arrived and assisted Tim with the anchor rode from his dinghy. The sea animal suddenly surfaced underneath Don's dinghy. We all realized then that it was a huge manta ray. Don's ten-and-a-half foot dinghy was on top of the ray. The ray's fins were sticking up above the water, a few feet away from either end of the dinghy showing that it was at least sixteen feet wide, if not more. Tim dove continually for the next ten minutes, wrestling his way to the tangled anchor rode while Neener was towed around between the anchored boats.

The Manta Ray took a dive under Neener taking Tim with him. I felt the ray hit the rudder. Neener was now moving towards another boat called Shiriri and then stopped. Tim surfaced and said that the ray was lying on the bottom with the anchor rode wrapper around one of its horns (properly called cephalic fins). Meanwhile, those of us on board were getting desperate. We found a large fender in a cockpit locker, attached it to the anchor rode and made ready to cast off. Then Tim dove twenty-seven feet to the bottom where he found the ray resting. To get a grip, Tim put his hand in the ray's mouth and was able to unwrap the chain off the horn. The now happy manta ray swam away. We found out later that Neener had been anchored with one hundred feet of chain and an equal amount of rope in twenty-seven feet of water. The ray had tangled the chain where it was shackled to the rope.

Just as we were pulling up the anchor, the owner of Neener returned from the beach in a state of shock. They had seen their boat moving away with people on board and a crowd of dinghies milling around it. We were happy to turn over the command of their boat all safe and sound. All's well that ends well!

JOANNA'S JOURNAL

Joshua, Dad and Tim were heroes of this amazing day!

Interestingly, for me, it was at this point that I was started to find the cruising life very wearisome. Tenacatita was the dream anchorage that we finally arrived to. It had taken us months to get there. We were in paradise and I was becoming more and more unhappy. There was hard work to do continually. For me there was no rest. I was making three large meals every day, cleaning up continually, overviewing the children and their schoolwork, and supporting Allan. Emotionally I was drained. The manta ray adventure took its toll on me. What else was going to happen?

There was no break in the routine. There was no break in the vigilance necessary in keeping our family safe and the boat maintained. Living on a boat with a family of five takes a great deal of patience, focus, energy, and self-control.

And in such tight quarters I was starting to feel severely claustrophobic and stuck. Everyone else on the boat seemed to be doing well. For our children it was a "cozy" place to be. They had all mastered the tenders and could sail, row or motor around whenever and wherever they wanted in the anchorage. Even Lydia could now start the Avon inflatable's motor on her own. I couldn't. I felt completely trapped with no way to get off the boat and no time to get off even if I wanted to. For Allan, he was living the dream.

We were seven months into our travels and it dawned on me; I was ready to go home.

Once I realized that was the problem I had, I perked up completely. I knew the reason for my growing unease and unhappiness and knew how to solve it.

The question was, how and when to break the news to Allan. His heart was set on circumnavigation. He had worked hard to make this trip work for us. He had planned it for years.

I kept my thoughts to myself.

Meanwhile, we had many miles to still travel.

I decided that one year on the boat was going to be enough. We would have accomplished what we wanted, and I just needed to find the right time to speak to Allan about it.

My despondency lifted.

The days pass happily with me wherever my ship sails.

—*Joshua Slocum*

CHAPTER 26

Mexican Riviera

South of Puerto Vallarta is the Mexican Riviera or the Mexican Gold Coast. It is a beautiful cruising ground during the winter months. The winds are moderate and the overall climate is pleasant. The small towns are charming and the beaches are spectacular. The distances between anchorages are not large and we enjoyed heading south to Melaque and Barre de Navidad for a few weeks.

Melaque and Barre de Navidad are picturesque coastal Mexican towns where we enjoyed eating at small kitchen cafés, shopping in the open markets, and travelling the local buses. We had our teeth cleaned by Dr. Pimienta Woo, a local Mexican dentist, who received his training in the States.

We anchored in Melaque Bay first. It is called "Rocky Melaque" by cruisers because of the large ocean swells that come in, sometimes causing a violent rocking motion of the boats. We enjoyed three nights there until the rolling really picked up. It was an easy thing to pick up anchor and go around the corner to the Barre de Navidad lagoon. The lagoon, while tricky to enter because it is narrow and shallow (cruisers kept getting grounded), was the calmest anchorage we had experienced in months. Completely flat seas, calm wind, and totally protected. It was a wonderful sensation to not be rolling at night. We slept deeply for those nights anchored in the lagoon. It was a refreshing respite.

Melaque had been a wonderful spot for swimming off of the boat. In contrast the lagoon appeared quite murky and we were hesitant to jump into the water. We weren't sure what unknowns would be under the surface.

Next to the lagoon there is a posh marina beside a luxury hotel. We knew a lot of cruisers who paid for moorage at the marina and they kindly invited us over every day to swim as their guests in the hotel pool. The hospitality we experienced among the cruisers was remarkable, and folks really wanted to care for our family.

Ginger and George, on the boat *Dalliance*, were particularly thoughtful. Both were amputees and managed their boat together with a total of two legs between them. What an amazing couple. George had designed Joshua's "ray rider" t-shirt. They had us visit their boat for snacks and insisted we swim in the pool with them during the afternoons.

A woman called Pam on a large motor yacht *Ocean Lady* was delighted to get to know us and when she found out Joanna's birthday was soon, she put on a lovely surprise birthday dinner with hamburgers, chocolate brownies, fruit cake, chips, balloons, and presents. Pam invited other cruisers to join us. It was a beautiful evening and our sensitive Joanna was delighted.

JOANNA'S JOURNAL

Happy birthday to me! Yeap, it's my birthday. I'll tell you what we did. I woke up and faced a delicious breakfast of sourdough pancakes and presents from the family. Joshua gave me the pen I'm writing with. It's a shiny green one with purple hearts on it. Lydia gave me a pile!: 2 stuffed animals, a bag which you put your book in with a matching pen, notepad and bookmark, a decoration pillow that said "school" on it, a book, a pouch with a matching pencil and eraser. Mom gave me pancakes and Dad gave me—well you'll see! We went out for a surprise lunch in town. Then we went shopping until 2 pm which is time to go to the pool. Then, guess what? We had a surprise party on Ocean Lady. It was a totally surprise and it was a lot of fun. I picked the music, we had appetizers, delicious hamburgers and the stuff to go with them and of course dessert. I got a lot of presents, because Pam asked other cruisers to come. We had so much fun! Best birthday ever!

On two occasions we saw the cruising community swing into action. Tim on *Treopia*, the diver who had freed the manta ray, came into the lagoon and got grounded. In no time every dinghy in the anchorage zoomed over to his assistance. The boat was floated off of the shallow spot into deeper water.

The second occasion involved our boat while we were away at the marina/ hotel pool swimming. Another boat had not anchored correctly and had swung into the side of our boat. Lots of cruisers saw this happen and quickly responded. Many boaters placed their zodiacs between the two boats to act as fenders and to prevent any damage. We were alerted by cruisers in the marina and Allan raced out on our inflatable to help untangle the anchor rodes that had wrapped up together. A number of men helped Allan to reset our anchor.

We returned for another night in Melaque so we could meet friends at Flor's, a family owned restaurant, for Pozole (maize and chicken soup) and then walk in the plaza. Cruisers and local Mexican families filled the plaza and strolled on this Sunday evening. This is a weekly tradition. It was cool and pleasant; a wonderful way to socialize and visit. The Mexican families dressed up their children in their Sunday best and we loved meeting them and taking their photos. Since we were travelling with our three children, we easily made relationships. Our children were an invitation to conversation, kindness and hospitality. The Mexicans were very welcoming to us as a family.

One afternoon in Melaque we had a cruising family on board visiting us. The Mexican navy came into the bay and randomly decided to board all of the boats to verify everyone's documentation. It was rather intimidating to have eight well-armed soldiers motor up to our boat. Our children, however, were impressed with the machine guns. The officer that boarded our boat was extremely courteous. After checking all of our paperwork we had a pleasant visit with him for half an hour and he didn't want to leave. It was a little nerve-wracking to see his gun pointed downwards and we subconsciously prayed it wouldn't go off. A hole in our boat would not be a good thing. We gave him some candy for his men, a Canadian flag pin, a Canadian polar bear postcard, and a Canadian pencil. He was so pleased with these little gifts that he gave us his name, address and phone number if we ever needed assistance. We learned that a little goodwill and sharing goes a long way.

JOSHUA'S JOURNAL

January 21: Now in Melaque and we went to the dentist in the morning! He cleaned our teeth! Dad went first! We came back for lunch and a rest. We invited some cruisers for dinner. Meanwhile the Mexican Navy boarded our boat!! The Lieutenant was very courteous and polite. He just wanted to check our ship's paper. Dad got into quite an animated conversation with him. He stayed for a long time!

January 27: We are in the lagoon at Barre Navidad. We love going to visit our friends on Dalliance, who are docked at the marina. George (I call him Mr. George) had a T-shirt made for me!!! It says RAY RIDER on it and on the back there is a picture of a manta ray towing a person on a surfboard! And the person is saying "Neener, Neener, Neener"!!

JOANNA'S JOURNAL

A travel day today from Barra back to Tenacatita. Everyone kept saying "WELCOME HOME!! I feel the same way!

As Joanna mentions in her journal entry we left Melaque and Barra De Navidad to return north to Tenacatita. We stayed for a couple of weeks, and met even more cruisers as the bay was filling up.

What was shocking to hear from the Tenacatita cruisers was that while we were away a large motor-yacht had caught on fire and completely burned to the waterline. This was a horrible situation but fortunately no one was hurt. The owners of the boat all jumped into the water while they watched their boat burn up.

I am so thankful our family did not see or witness that disaster. The news of the boat fire strengthened my resolve to return home at the end of the cruising season. I prayed for the right opportunity to speak with Allan. That chance did not come for many weeks.

We continued north.

Chamela is a small town north of Tenacatita and part of the beautiful, uncrowded Gold Coast. We had sailed past it on our overnight on Christmas Eve to Tenacatita. It was an ideal stop as we travelled north on our way back to Puerto Vallarta.

JOANNA'S JOURNAL

We left for Chamela early in the morning. It was kind of over-cast at first but then the sun showed its cheerful face and pushed away the clouds leaving an empty blue sky. We caught a fish first thing- it was a messy one! We had blood everywhere! It was flipping around a lot. Nothing else happened, except that I felt rather sick! We arrived in Chamela an hour after lunch. When you look out to sea from Chamela the sight is very pretty. The water is an aqua colour- like in a magazine! And there is a very picturesque island.

Chamela was in a somewhat exposed bay with large ocean swells coming into it. The dinghy landings were very difficult here and it was the one place where we flipped the dinghy and fell into the water with all our things. Timing is everything with surf landings, and we miscalculated. Fortunately it was so warm out that we didn't mind getting soaked and we dried out quickly.

The beach at Chamela is six miles long. Somehow we never tired of walking miles of empty beaches. It was a great way to use up excess energy... specifically, the children's! Between swimming and walking our kids slept well at night.

This was one place where we met a number of other children. A motor-yacht called *Onawa* had three children aboard and for two hours one afternoon their family offered to tow our children around the bay on kneeboards. This was a new experience for us and all three of our children were enthusiastic to try. The wind was up to 15 knots directly into the anchorage, but that didn't deter any of them. It was choppy, but Joshua and his friend Cooper managed to stand up on their boards. Even our little Lydia insisted on having a turn. We were continually amazed at the skills

Joshua, Joanna, and Lydia were developing around the water. It was deeply rewarding for Allan and me to watch such growing independence and fearlessness.

LYDIA'S JOURNAL

We walked the beach at Chamela with a family from the boat Onawa. Our surf landing was another thing. We got as close to flipping as you can get. The boat filled with sand and saltwater. Onawa (they had 3 children) helped us bail out the water and lift up the dinghy. We just about wrecked our motor.

Land was created to provide a place for boats to visit.
—*Brooks Atkinson*

CHAPTER 27

Puerto Vallarta

Puerto Vallarta was the largest Mexican city we visited. It has a population of 200,000 and is a popular tourist destination. On our return to Puerto Vallarta, my parents made arrangements to visit us for a second time. We were so excited!

To get to Puerto Vallarta we had to "bash" north so called because it is sailing against the prevailing winds and waves. Breaking up the trip from Tenacatita to Chamela and then Chamela to Puerto Vallarta made the trip more manageable. It was comforting to round Cape Corrientes and to sail into familiar protected Banderas Bay. Puerto Vallarta is at the end of the huge bay.

JOSHUA'S JOURNAL

Before we arrive to Puerto Vallarta we anchor in front of little town called La Cruz in Banderas Bay. A lot of our cruising friends anchor there and it is a great little Mexican town to visit before arriving to the big city of Puerto Vallarta. Today we had an interesting experience in La Cruz. Early in the morning we went into the town and walked through the streets. We saw a cow being butchered in someone's garage. It looked pretty messy. But this is the kind of thing we see around here. There was a flea market selling many things and we wandered through it. We went to the primary school and the secondary school. At the primary school the girls were wearing gingham dresses, and the boys in blue shorts and white shirts. I like the uniforms down here.

Later we walked to a tortillaria and bought fresh corn tortillas (we have learned that they don't taste very good the next day!). We had these for lunch. It was quite difficult to get back to the boat in the big surf.

Puerto Vallarta is a very convenient spot for cruisers. It is an easy place to provision, refuel, work on boat maintenance, and socialize. There are three marinas to choose from and a large supportive cruising community. The airport is nearby so family and friends can visit. It is also where the South Pacific yearly "fleet" make their final preparations to leave for the Marqueses in French Polynesia at 2,800 nautical miles away.

Our Amigo Net was still going strong and became a lifeline for all who checked in as they travelled up and down the coastline. Allan and I frequently ran the Amigo Net in the mornings and we found it a very helpful way to stay in touch with the folks we met. Our propagation on *Morning* was so good that we were able to chat daily with up to 10 boats who were doing the South Pacific crossing and relay their messages. We could travel vicariously through them. As a result many other cruisers began to listen and check in to our Net as we could relay messages for them.

A weather man, Don Anderson on sailing vessel *Summer Passage* began to check in, giving all of us extensive up-to-date weather coverage. He was able to give plenty of warning when Hurricane Aletta developed, for example. A number of our friends made dramatic changes in plans since they would have crossed the hurricane track. Don continued to give weather advice for the next 12 years, and we heard that in 2012 he passed away. What an amazing service he provided for thousands of cruisers for over a decade on the Amigo Net that we had started! Everyone who listened learned and benefitted from his vast weather expertise gained from NOAA, the largest USA weather agency.

Heading into the end of our season we were amazed at the number of people who had checked into the Amigo Net. We would have up to 20 check-ins a day with vessels underway as far away as San Francisco, San Diego, Baja, mainland Mexico (west coast), El Salvador, Guatemala, Costa Rica, Galapagos Islands, Marqueses, and Tuomotus in French Polynesia. The radio had become a significant part of our cruising lifestyle. It was comforting to know that we could communicate while cruising, since we were often travelling long distances on the ocean alone.

In Puerto Vallarta for a second time, we enjoyed relaxing and being tourists with my parents. Joshua was thrilled to try parasailing at grandpa's suggestion. It was also a good time for the children to get a lot of schoolwork done. Joanna completed her novel, *The Mangrove Secret* and we sent lots of mail, newsletters, and school work home with my parents. It was a productive time for all of us.

Since we were at a dock at Nuevo Vallarta, we had easy access to shore. We loved going on long walks every day. There was a beach to walk on, as well as a small town close by with an open market. We thoroughly enjoyed the once-a-week market day and were able to buy a lot of fresh fruit, vegetables, and meat at reasonable prices.

JOANNA'S JOURNAL

Gram and Grandpa are coming tomorrow. We had to get ready for them so we did schoolwork as hard as we could! So we could send back lots, and I mean TONS with Gram. We did laundry too! What a job! Anyways we got everything done and ready to have a holiday with them!

Puerto Vallarta
Puerto Vallarta's a noisy town,
The roar of the buses heading downtown,
The busy people running around,
Pushing and shoving with a lot of sound;
Mexicans shouting,
Money exchangers counting;
The traffic on the roads.

The shoppers laden with their daily loads,
The yellow taxi cabs passing by,
Filled with tourists on the fly.
The roughness of the cobblestones,

The buses jolt with grunts and groans,
Along the streets people dance and sing,
Everyone trying to sell you something.
Savoury smells from the stands,
Food to satisfy your demands,
Bananas that are roasted,
And tacos that are toasted.

On it goes day after day and night after night!

I haven't recorded the fun time we had with Gram and Grandpa, but
I can tell you we've had a great time! What with a huge meals 3 times
a day (very good) and snacks plus drinks in between. Me and Dad are
getting pretty good at the surf kayaking. Joshua got to go para sailing-
lucky! We had just a really great time. Gram and Grandpa left yesterday.
I was very sad! There was just so much to do that I really cannot explain
it all! Anyways, I can't remember most of it! But now, we're back to plain
boat meals. They're really not that bad, just the cereal (oatmeal) for
breakfast- Yuck! Its Sunday today and guess what? We came home late
last night and discovered our boat has cock roaches! Lydia was freaked
out but I don't really care! Boat life again!

JOSHUA'S JOURNAL

When Gram and Grandpa came to visit us in Puerto Vallarta, Grandpa
let me go parasailing. It was so exciting!! As soon as the harness was
attached and the motorboat pulled me forward I rose quite fast. I just
sat still and felt like a leaf fluttering in the breeze. And oh, it was still and
quiet way up there. The view was tremendous. Landing was a little scary. I
pulled the rope too soon that is used to land. It spilled the air and I dove
down to the side. It looked like I was going to hit the Hotel! I didn't and it
was a very special treat. I thanked Grandpa.

LYDIA'S JOURNAL

In the morning we did school work. Saucy Lady came over and we went sailing in 25 knot winds. Up ahead there was 100's of birds diving ahead of us. There we saw a whale mother teaching her baby to slap its tail. We were about 10 feet away from the whale. We were surrounded by diving birds. We healed way over and had a nice sail. When we got back to La Cruz we had soup, quesadillas, tea and cookies. We had a nice visit.

There are three sorts of people: those who are alive, those
who are dead, and those who are at sea.

—*Old Capstan Chantey attributed to Anacharsis, 6th century BC*

CHAPTER 28

Captain Norm

We continued our trip north from Puerto Vallarta to revisit our favourite little
town of Chacala. We stayed for a couple of days. We revisited the school and
the children and teachers were keen to see us again. We were asked to help
the students compose and write thank you letters in English to an elementary
school in the USA that had sent them things. It was fun to encourage the
children to try and speak English as they wrote out each word.

LYDIA'S JOURNAL

In the morning at Chacala, we went ashore and walked the beach. When
we came back to where we put our dinghy, the pangas (Mexican open
fishing boats) were all in the way so we just talked with some cruisers (with
2 children). We talked and fed the pelicans until the pangas moved. We
got 2 inches away from the pelicans by holding out small left over fish!

We continued north to San Blas, a very old Mexican town that had
originally been a fort in the 1700s. There were few tourists there. And we
soon learned why. We had to cross a narrow, shallow bar to get into the
estuary that bordered on the town. Captain Norm used light signals to direct
us over the bar, as he did for every cruiser visiting. However we only cleared
the shoal by one foot and that was at high slack tide. We would have never
made it over the bar without Captain Norm's help.

When we anchored in the estuary there wasn't a lot of room for many boats. Getting on and off the boat was a challenge because a strong current ran through the lagoon/estuary. This was also the first time in our trip that we experienced serious bugs. It was buggy! Tiny no-see-ums snuck through any opening into our boat. Allan and Lydia were all but eaten alive. We were thankful for the screens I had sewn for our opening windows and hatches. The only disadvantage was that the air circulation became minimal and it got hot and stuffy inside the cabin.

Visiting Captain Norm was our main reason for stopping in San Blas, so we spent very little time on our boat and enjoyed the ambiance of this historical town. Captain Norm ran the San Blas Fisherman and Cruiser's Net in the early evenings and did a remarkable promotion of San Blas. He encouraged every cruiser to stop in. We were sure that he was responsible for a significant amount of tourist dollars coming into this unique little Mexican town. We didn't want to miss it.

We had three days in San Blas. It was another Mexican immersion experience. We had meals out for $5 each, eating traditional Mexican food. For example, we found a wonderful fish taco stand where we had dinner.

JOANNA'S JOURNAL

We walked out of town to find a suitable restaurant. We found a little place where they smoked fish on the spot. It was so so good! The funny thing was, that the whole block had restaurants exactly the same!

We hiked up the main hill to the very old San Blas fort and church. What a fabulous view of the ocean. We found the main plaza where locals gather and met. We wandered through the crowds and saw a parade of small children dressed up to celebrate springtime.

The highlight of San Blas was meeting the remarkable Captain Norm Goldie and his pretty wife Janet. They are two Americans who had settled and lived in San Blas for 34 years. This couple made a point of assisting cruisers. We learned a great deal from them. They are true characters.

Captain Norm was a huge overweight man and his wife was tiny. Captain Norm had a wealth of nautical experience and knowledge and shared with whoever would listen. Every night he ran the Net and he encouraged cruisers to volunteer to take net control (the radio station that manages the traffic on the net) and he would give the weather report, which we as cruisers relied on. Joshua eagerly took net control a number of times and as a result, Captain Goldie presented Joshua with a certificate of thanks and a seamanship book.

JOSHUA'S JOURNAL

March 18: We arrived at Matenchan Bay at 6 pm and dropped the hook. At 5:30 pm I started the San Blas Fisherman's and Cruiser's Net. This was my first time being net control for this net. I really enjoyed it!

March 19: We moved over to the estuary with the guidance of Captain Norm Goldie. He and his wife, Mrs. Janet, are Americans and he gives the weather for the San Blas Fishermen's Net.

March 20: We met the Goldie's at their house and Captain Norm gave me a certificate of thanks for doing the net (also a nautical emergency book). It was awfully generous of them!!

The Goldies were a beautifully hospitable people and insisted we visit them in their home. It was a tiny place, full of antiques and nicknacks. We signed their autograph book. We gave them our children's writings, some Canadian pencils, and Joshua's manta ray story that he had sent in to *Latitude 38* magazine. The Goldies were delighted to meet our three children. It was a highlight for them. While we visited, other cruisers popped by, dropping off clothes for the poor, since the Goldies assisted the locals in the town in many ways, and also distributed financial donations. They had a busy home. Janet had her drawings and paintings on display. As a proficient artist she loved to create detailed, intricate portraits of the locals in the community.

After listening to Captain Norm on the radio most days while in Mexico, it was wonderful to actually meet him and his wife in person. In our years of preparation for our trip south, we had heard of Captain Norm from other experienced cruisers. As an old-timer, Captain Norm helped make cruising in Mexico safer. What a privilege to meet this big-hearted generous man.

All things bright and beautiful
All creatures great and small,
All things wise and wonderful:
The Lord God made them all.

—Cecil Alexander

CHAPTER 29

Booby Birds

Our bash north against wind and waves continued as we headed 40 miles to Isla Isabela, the site of Jacques Cousteau documentaries and a former research station. Leaving San Blas estuary was tricky and we had to time our departure with high slack tide. We were relieved to leave the bugs and get into the fresh clear ocean air. The wind was 20 knots directly on the nose of the boat. The seas got large. It was difficult to motor in those conditions so we had to sail, tacking back and forth to minimize the bashing. We had 40 miles to travel to Isla Isabella, if we went in a straight line.

Leaving San Blas at 10:30 we arrived at the island at dark. Perfect timing. It was good to return to this spot and the rolling didn't bother us at all since we had had such a bumpy ride up to the anchorage. It is amazing what you get use to. We knew where the "rock" was that we needed to avoid, having recorded positions on the GPS from our previous visit, and our anchor held firmly. The wind was strong in the anchorage but there were no waves, so it was comfortable. Allan put up the riding sail to keep the boat from swinging back and forth. It worked well.

The delight was getting ashore next morning. On our first trip to Isla Isabella in November we were afraid to leave our boat. This time we made it. Isla Isabella has similarities to the famous Galapagos Islands off of Ecuador because the same species and varieties of birds are found in both places. We hiked up to the lighthouse hill and birds were everywhere. Nests, chicks and eggs. It was a giant bird nursery. We saw blue-footed boobies, yellow-footed boobies, gulls, and frigate birds. We were able to see eggs, babies in various stages, and nests close-up. Allan took amazing photos. We had to be careful where we stepped, so we tiptoed around the island trying to avoid upsetting the nesting mothers and to not step on the camouflaged eggs. Isa Isabella is an extraordinary place. For the children it was an experience of a life-time to see such a variety of birds, nests and eggs. This was interactive wilderness.

JOANNA'S JOURNAL

A day to see the wonderful Isla Isabella. It is very famous because Jacques Cousteau did a documentary on the birds. The island is a bird nesting place. We saw tons of gecko's, lizards and huge iguanas. We proceeded up the hill. At first we saw hundreds of frigate birds with their chicks. They were very cute and would smack their beaks together when you got too close to them. Still, we were able to get very close to them! Next came the boobies. The neat thing about them was their sky blue feet! Some had yellow feet, some had green feet and some had purple feet! They also made very funny noises. These birds also had their chicks and even eggs. It was very neat! Even the red beaked gulls laid brown speckled eggs!

The Island of Birds
The grass is dry and brown,
Away-far away lies the island of birds,
Where the wind blows strong,
Away-far away lies the island of birds,
All the frigates and gulls packed in a throng,
They dwell on this island of birds.
The gulls and their speckled eggs in the nest,
That's what you will find on the island of birds,
The boobies and their chicks near at rest,
They cover that island of birds.

The frigates of black and white,
Also, on the island of birds,
all comical and a funny sight,
It all covers the island of birds.

It's a wonderful place this island of birds.

LYDIA'S JOURNAL

At Isla Isabella we got ready to go ashore. There was no surf at the beach we landed at. When we got ashore we walked up the hill and saw blue footed boobies, blue footed boobie babys, yellowfooted boobies with babys, green footed boobies with babys, some kind of gull, frigates with babys and lots more... There are 100s of birds up here. Watch where you step because there is a few nests with eggs! The blue footed boobie chicks are very soft and white. Don't get too near them because the mothers and fathers get very upset.

There is but a plank between a sailor and eternity.

—*Thomas Gibbons*

CHAPTER 30
Gunnel to Gunnel

After a couple of magical days on Isla Isabella we sailed 80 more miles to the city of Mazatlan. We left at 05:30 on Friday, March 24. We planned on arriving at dusk into the large, well-marked harbour. It started off as quite a lumpy trip but settled out as the wind died down and the swell lessened. It was a beautiful day, and as the wind swung around enough we were able to put the sails up and enjoy some good sailing. By dusk the wind began to drop so we started the engine.

We were 15 miles from the Mazatlan harbour entrance. Allan started the engine and shifted into gear… "Grind… thud!" The engine was not sounding right. Allan checked the fuel system. He tried again but the vibration on everything was terrible when putting the engine into gear. Something was definitely wrong. After checking out what he could, Allan realized that the prop was fouled; something was wrapped around the propeller so that it would not turn. The engine would run but we had no propulsion whatsoever.

By this time it was dark, and with a heavy swell running and the stern of the boat heaving up and down smacking the water, it was out of the question to go overboard to work on the propeller. We had to put the sails up and try to sail to Mazatlan Harbour. We tacked back and forth a lot but made no headway into the 8 knots of NW wind. On my watch (23:00–02:00) we set course away from land to give us a better direction to sail to the harbour. At 02:00 the wind died completely, so Allan brought in the sails and we rocked back and forth, gunnel to gunnel for the next five hours until 07:00. We had no choice but to drift and roll in the short heaving swell. We rolled and pitched violently with no sails and no engine, waiting for daybreak. It was the most sickening, miserable, and relentless motion.

And we could do nothing about it.

My consolation was that our friends crossing the South Pacific were experiencing the same conditions. My other consolation was that our children did not complain or get seasick.

No seasickness. No complaining.

Amazing.

During the evening Allan was on the VHS radio speaking in Spanish, warning the Mexican fishing fleet that we were motorless just offshore of the Mazatlan Harbour. It was not a call for help, but we wanted to warn vessels that we were an obstacle in their way as they approached the harbour entrance. I am thankful for Allan's fluency in Spanish, and apparently a lot of boaters, cruisers, and even the Mexican lighthouse keeper heard Allan's calls.

By 07:00 Allan was under the pitching boat to check the propeller. He put on a wetsuit because the water was cold. He held his breath to dive down under our deep hull. As it turned out we had snagged a pair of men's heavy work pants on the propeller. They were very tightly wound around the prop and shaft. It took a great deal of effort for Allan to cut them free one small piece at a time, using a razor-sharp knife. It was exhausting work in cold water with a pitching boat overhead. Since we hadn't slept all night, Allan found it hard to focus and complete the task. Joshua and I were in the cockpit watching Allan closely. Allan had a rope tied around his waist so that we could pull him aboard if he got knocked out by our crashing boat.

Joshua and I prayed out loud. This was a serious situation. We could do nothing but pray. It was frightening to think of what could happen because we knew at any point, with any wave, the boat could come crashing down on Allan and smash his skull and body. We concentrated on watching Allan's every move so that we could give him warning when the larger sets of waves came along.

What a huge relief when Allan bobbed to the surface with a large piece of the pants in his hands to show us. He sluggishly struggled to climb back into our rolling boat and went to start the engine.

It ran perfectly and he pointed Morning directly to Mazatlan Harbour. We had 20 miles to motor. Allan went straight to his bunk, shivering violently. We wrapped him up in sleeping bags and Joshua and I steered the boat to the harbour entrance.

By now, we were thankful to come into the harbour during daylight. It was an easy entry and we dropped the hook in front of Club Nautico inside the harbour breakwater.

It felt wonderful to be in a quiet place that did not rock and roll and that had no bugs. We all napped for a few hours.

What an ordeal… that lasted ALL night!

It was the worst night of our trip.

Allan now had doubts about circumnavigating. For the first time he had a question in his mind. Could we do it? Could he do it? Should we do it?

JOANNA'S JOURNAL

We had something wrapped around our propeller. So there was no going into the harbour, instead we spent a miserable night bobbing around outside the harbour entrance!

We got there at last! HAPPY BIRTHDAY!! It was Dad's birthday and we celebrated it by a huge brunch!

We became deeply appreciative for the simple, quiet, good things in life. Our perspective had significantly changed. One bad night and we saw our boating experience in a very different light.

Cruising has two pleasures. One is to go out in wider waters from a sheltered place. The other is to go into a sheltered place from wider waters.

—*Howard Bloomfield*

CHAPTER 31

Mazatlan

Our week in Mazatlan was really enjoyable. It was a refreshing break from sailing. It became one of our most memorable stops of the year.

We anchored in the harbour and had easy access to a dinghy dock at Club Nautico where there was 24-hour security. There were hot showers, which was a wonderful luxury. Most cruisers stay at marinas, but throughout our year we chose to anchor out most of the time. This made the trip challenging but more financially feasible. Learning to anchor out and get ashore was all part of the adventure and the children adapted naturally to it.

Mazatlan is a charming city to walk and explore, particularly the Old Town. It felt European-like with narrow cobble streets, colourful stucco buildings, plazas, and ornate churches. It is historic and did not have many tourists. We found the huge central mercado. It sold a wide variety of fruit, vegetables, meat, and fish which was the best choice on our trip. I was delighted to buy broccoli for the first time in months.

On our first day in Mazatlan we hiked up to the lighthouse, the second highest natural lighthouse in the world. It is a remarkable light which had given me great comfort to watch when we were rocking and rolling 20 miles offshore in the middle of the night without wind and without engine.

And what a fabulous view of Mazatlan and the coastline.

Allan had an animated chat in Spanish with the lighthouse keeper. He had heard Allan on our radio calling in the middle of the night when Allan was trying to alert the fishing fleet of our presence in front of the harbour entrance. He was very happy to meet our family and know we were safe.

That evening we enjoyed the peace and quiet with no rolling. Allan read Shakespeare to the children while they cuddled up together in the centre berth. Reading continued to be a hugely significant part of what we did on board. The children loved being read to and consequently became voracious readers themselves. These were sweet times together. After surviving through our all night ordeal, the calm afterwards was relished and enjoyed all the more.

Mazatlan was another Mexican immersion experience for us. Chacala had been our first immersion experience in a small seaside village. Mazatlan was the second, but was the large city version. We found a more activities to do here than anywhere we had been. Every day we had full days in town exploring.

Each day started and ended with the radio, checking in first to the Amigo Net, then in the evening to the San Blas Fisherman's and Cruiser's Net. It gave a framework to our day. I enjoyed reporting our activities to the cruisers who were underway.

There was documentation and paperwork to complete in Mexico and it took a full week of going back and forth to the Customs office to do it all. In order to stay longer in Mexico we had to import our boat. Allan's Spanish came in handy and he really enjoyed the exercise of completing a surprisingly tedious process. The authorities, who often do not speak English, appreciated Allan speaking Spanish to them. At the end of it all, we presented Canadian pencils to two of the women who assisted us—they really appreciated the gesture.

We visited the Grand Mercado which was the main farmer's market in the heart of town. The mercado is huge and we were aghast to see so much fresh produce, whole carcasses of beef, pork and chicken displayed aisle after aisle in this giant warehouse. There was fresh fish, local cheese, fresh hot bakery items. There were racks of colorful hand-stitched embroidered clothing, kitchenware, trinkets, blankets, plants, and almost anything else you could think. It was a grand local "one stop shop."

We did not see anyone else other than Mexicans shopping there in the Grand Mercado.

We discovered tiny local eateries upstairs where we enjoyed lunch in a little Mexican kitchen. There was a stove, sink and small counter where the mamas cooked their basic bean, rice, chicken, or fish dishes. There were two plastic covered tables with benches. We paid a few pesos for a hot meal.

We found the main church with its plaza, as well as other smaller plazas dotted among the narrow winding streets.

We walked the seawall that lined the Old Town and enjoyed the scenic viewpoints along the way, including a spot where men dove off a high rock.

Next, it was a jump onto a local bus to visit the Mazatlan Aquarium. Even though it was quite a small venue, it was a lot of fun to visit. Well-attended by Mexican families, we stood out as the one gringo family. There were numerous tanks filled with a wide variety of local fish from Mexico as well as a display area for turtles, a large tank for piranhas, a shark pool, a very cute seal and sea lion performance, and a bird show. As a family, engaging in a family place with Mexican families, it made us feel like we were part of their community.

LYDIA'S JOURNAL

In Mazatlan we took the bus to the aquarium. We went to all the shows. At the sea lion show the sea lions danced with their trainer, jumped high, kissed everyone and did a lot of other tricks. At the diving exhibition the diver swims with two very large sharks and four big turtles.

At the bird show there were about 7 parrots that did tricks like riding a small bike, doing a puzzle, talking and a lot of other things. Then we went to the alligator pond and Dad touched an alligator! There was also small turtles in the pond. In the building there was all kinds of fish: shiny angelfish, boxfish, damselfish, morey eel, puffer fish, prawns, cat fish, dog fish, red snapper, sharks, turtles, tiger fish, lion fish, octopus, longnose angelfish, king angel, tang fish and lots more...then we took the bus back to the boat.

We found a local whole wheat bakery for the first time in Mexico which is unusual since the tortilla is the mainstay food for the country. We bought cinnamon buns, bread and meat pastries. This was indulgence... and how we savoured them!

In the Old Town we discovered an archeological museum. Just past it was the Mother Theresa primary school. The schools were all locked and gated in the cities, this one included. We stood at the front gate however, and a group of little girls came up to the gate, along with their teacher. They sang to us, introduced themselves in English, grinned and laughed. They were charming in their little uniforms of blue skirts, white blouses, red bows. All the girls were very pretty with their long black hair tied back in ribbons. Our children attracted other children and we had immediate acceptance into the schools local community wherever we went. We enjoyed these interactions greatly, because they were spontaneous and genuine.

The theatre had a Gala Year End Ballet production that we managed to get tickets for on the last night. We attended it with some other cruisers and it was a real treat. This was a small taste of civilization that I had been missing.

Allan heard about two interesting 400-year-old mining towns that were inland in the hills. He thought this would be an unusual experience to travel by local bus to explore these towns. We were up early on a Sunday morning and bussed out of Mazatlan. The main feature of both towns were the 200-year-old churches and open plazas in front of them. Even though it was Sunday and the churches were open, no one was in them. We continued to wander and explore, enjoying the cooler climate, taking in the views of the rural farmlands. We met a pastor who warned us to be careful in our travels, since the area was full of bandits. I found this a bit disconcerting, and was relieved when we made our way back to Mazatlan. As it was Sunday, there was no return bus so we got rides in small open pickup trucks with wood benches.

JOANNA'S JOURNAL

We had a lot fun today! At 6:30 am (very early for us) we were on a bus heading for town! We got off at the bus terminal, ready for a day trip to Copala! It was a three hour bus trip there and lots of fun! Once we got to the old mining town of Copala we were shown right into the town. It's a very quaint tiny little town. We had a look at two very nice restaurants and a cute tiny hotel. There was a shop with interesting Mexican arts, crafts, and silver. After that I got to ride a donkey around the square, which was a lot of fun! We saw lots of pigs and even a donkey carrying a huge bundle of wood. We had lots of fun there. Next we ate lunch and took a taxi to the neighbouring town of Concordia. It was also very old. It was getting late so we decided to catch the bus back. In town we decided to either go out for dinner or go back to the boat, we ended up going back to the boat for a delicious dinner.

It was a full week in Mazatlan and there was provisioning to do so we could be ready to make our second crossing of the Sea of Cortez. We were following the weather reports on the Chubasco Net, another radio net we started to listen to and finally decided to leave on a Wednesday morning after hearing a five-day forecast that was good.

At sea, I learned how little a person needs, not how much.

—*Robin Lee Graham*

CHAPTER 32

The Sea of Cortez

We made the dreaded crossing of the Sea of Cortez in flat calm seas, motoring for 39 hours. Having the experience of our first crossing, we knew that it was an upwind course motoring directly into the wind. In a northerly blow these seas could get very steep and large. We had a very pleasant trip compared to our first crossing. The Sea was a clear sapphire blue. We saw dolphins, huge whales breaching and schools of small manta rays leaping and belly-flopping into the water (hence their nickname 'belly-floppers').

LYDIA'S JOURNAL

At 10:00 am we left for La Paz. It was really foggy and calm for the first few hours. The fog cleared and the wind picked up but it was on our nose so we couldn't sail. It is 200 miles to La Paz. A lot of other boats left at the same time we did. In the afternoon we saw little manta rays jump. I did my one hour watch in the afternoon. We also saw two very big whales breech lots of times but they were really far away. We also saw lots of dolphins up close.

We made a night landfall at Ballandra Bay, 18 miles out of La Paz. We normally avoided night landfalls, but it was not too scary with the radar and navigation lights showing San Lorenzo channel and we had friends in the anchorage who gave us GPS coordinates of their position over the radio before they went to sleep. Charted positions are sometimes a mile or more in error in Mexico, so getting accurate positions is critical. Everything went fine, except when a 20 knot wind developed suddenly in the channel when we were five miles out of the bay. We managed to anchor successfully in rather bouncy conditions.

Ballandra Bay is famous for its mushroom shaped rock. But we were particularly impressed with the clear turquoise green water and white sand beach. With the contrast against a deep blue sky it all felt like we could have been in the South Pacific.

The next day we headed for La Paz where we enjoyed a week of genuine Mexican ambience. A highlight here was watching Joshua have a conversation in Spanish with an older Mexican man. We realized that while studying Spanish for a school course, he was actually learning Spanish well enough to converse with the locals we met.

We enjoyed our regular visits to the farmer's markets, tortillarias, carnecerias or meat markets, and bakeries, searching for the bargains along the way. We were feeling at home in Mexico by this point making our way around the community like Mexican people do.

We anchored out at the virtual marina. "Virtual" because the marina part didn't exist yet. However, they had a good anchoring area and onshore amenities such as a dinghy dock, garbage pickup, hot showers, and—most importantly—a swimming pool. During the mornings the children did schoolwork while Allan and I did boat chores. We had lunch, a siesta then a swim at the pool. It was a pleasant routine. Also, since we were founders of the Amigo Net we were meeting a lot of cruisers as we travelled. They would listen to the Net, start to check in, and then we would meet them on their boats during our travels. In La Paz we met many "old friends" from the Net. We were part of a vibrant and helpful boat community that was becoming a significant part of our lives.

Since our radio propagation was so good, we were one of the few boats that could hear and be heard over large distances. This was due to Allan's hard work and diligence in figuring out the best way to wire our radio. We continued to keep in contact with the boats who were travelling across the Pacific to the Marqueses and the Tuamotos, in French Polynesia. We were amazed at the daily contact we had with our friends sailing that distance away. By the time cruisers arrived in the Tuamotos (3,600 miles away), we could no longer hear them. But, it did mean we could travel with them vicariously as they slowly made their way across that vast long stretch of ocean. For many of these boats, our daily check-in become very important and encouraging as that passage is long, lonely, and potentially frightening. Don Anderson, the weatherman, was giving accurate weather reports daily on the Amigo Net as well, and this led to the Net's popularity. Up to 30 boats were checking in everyday until we hauled our boat out of the water in San Carlos. We hoped the Net would continue over the years, and it was wonderful to us, to hear in 2019 (20 years later) that it was still going and was just as popular! As we continued to visit Mexico decades later and the Sea of Cortez, we met cruisers who told us the Amigo Net was still going strong.

It was during our week in La Paz that I had the chance to approach Allan about finishing our trip. With all the experiences of the last few months I was convinced that going home was the best plan. The gunnel to gunnel rolling event off of Mazatlan made it obvious to me that this lifestyle for our family was not sustainable. It is a romantic idea and dream for many, but the reality of living on a boat for an extended period of time is extremely difficult and challenging. And very few people do it with three children on board.

I broached the subject carefully with Allan while sitting in the cockpit. Our children were down below working on their school assignments. It was a shock to him that in six weeks our adventure could draw to a close. He was prepared to head towards San Carlos on the mainland for the boat to be hauled out for the summer. But he had hoped to return in the fall to continue on to the South Pacific. I was firm in my decision, while appreciating the fact that as skipper Allan needed time to process this new plan.

For the next five weeks we gunk-holed which meant making short hops in daylight from anchorage to anchorage, from La Paz north to Bahia Conception. Since we were out of the swell of the Pacific Ocean and the northerly winds were not blowing, we found that travelling in the Sea of Cortez was a sublime experience. With the warm weather it was cruising at its best. There were numerous spectacular anchorages that were not a great distance apart. The month of May was a wonderful time to travel in the Sea, as it was starting to warm up by this point. We planned our final destination to be at San Carlos, to arrive by the end of the month for boat haul-out and dry storage.

Starting from the provisioning port of La Paz, we travelled north and visited the following anchorages on the milk run, which is a route that the majority of cruisers take: Caleta Partida, Isla San Francisco, Los Gatos, Aqua Verde, a small hot springs cove north of Cosme Island, Candeleros South, Puerto Escondido, Ballandra Bay, Isla Coronados (a national park), San Juanico, and Bahia Conception. Los Gatos was the most beautiful anchorage, and Isla San Francico was the most spectacular. Both had clear turquoise green water, a white sand beach tucked into a bay lined with spectacular red and green rock formations. Los Gatos has brilliant red gigantic rocks that look like pillows billowing down to the water's edge.

Caleta Partida was our first anchorage outside of La Paz and was in the centre of a volcano crater. We stayed there for a full week because some strong northerly weather had developed and we felt there was no point in bashing our way north. It is a large bay and well protected, so it was a pleasant place to be anchored, albeit very windy. The children enjoyed dinghy sailing in up to 20 knots of wind. Another cruising boat arrived with children and they had a sailing dinghy, so there were dinghy races in the bay. The turquoise water was crystal clear and the snorkeling was excellent although the water was quite cool, so we wore two wetsuits one on top of the other.

JOSHUA'S JOURNAL

April 16: On our way to Caleta Partida. The seas were very calm leaving the La Paz harbour. When we rounded the point the wind increased up to 15 knots. Coming into this section of water we saw amazing land forms of the Baja! The land is very barren and covered with cactus. The cliffs to the water are all different colours and shapes. Very neat!

April 17: It is so quiet here in Caleta Partida!! The silence is profound. It is so peaceful. And the water is very clear to twenty feet!

April 20: Another boat had a sailing dinghy and children on board! We raced around the bay! It kind of reminded me of my favourite book series Swallows and Amazons.

LYDIA'S JOURNAL

In the morning we got up and went ashore at the beach at Caleta Partida. There was lots of dead manta rays. Their wings were made of lots of small flexible strong bones so that they could swim swiftly. There was also a few dried up octopuses and eels! I found a pair of jaw bones. I also got some teeth from a dead fish. They were surprisingly clean and white. The fishes teeth came out there is a new set of teeth already. When that comes out there is more teeth. We also found amazing shells and other dead animals. Such as puffer fish, and birds. There was little bugs like cockroaches climbing all over the wet rocks, so be careful.

Upon leaving Caleta Partida the watermaker stopped working. We were quite concerned because we were out of fresh water, and with no watermaker we would have to return to La Paz to fix it. It would have been impossible to visit the remote anchorages in the Sea without fresh water on board, and there was no place to get any en route. Thankfully, because Allan had installed all the equipment on the boat he had ideas on what to check for. He discovered we had a defective ten cent fuse under our sleeping area. Allan replaced it and voila! The watermaker worked.

On our way to Isla San Francisco we made water, filling up every container we had on board. I marvelled that Allan could consistently find and fix things as they broke on our boat.

JOSHUA'S JOURNAL

We had a lovely motor sail from Caleta Partida to Isla San Francisco! Dad ran the watermaker and filled up our tanks. Isla San Francisco was unreal! A whole cliff on one side of the island was entirely green intermingled with brilliant reds and browns. Stunning! In the green rocks agates can sometimes be found. We anchored and the water was so clear! So turquoise and clear, we could easily see our anchor lying on the bottom!

JOANNA'S JOURNAL

We're underway again! We left Isla San Francisco for Los Gatos. We passed the volcano cliffs and cactus strewn land. The air is at a warm temperature and everything is perfect. We got into the anchorage, put on our snorkel gear and went for a snorkel in the kelp, it was the best!

Aqua Verde is a secure, protected anchorage with lots of snorkeling spots, especially around Roca Solitaria, a huge pinnacle rock dotted with heron nests off the entrance of the bay. We saw the largest variety of fish, starfish, sea cucumbers, coral and fan seaweed there. There were schools of wrasse, angelfish, damselflies, needlefish, large colourful parrot fish, hogfish, and sergeant majors. We saw a small octopus and moray eels. The water was remarkably clear and we could see to great depths. The water was also much warmer and we could stay in the water a lot longer without getting chilled, and without wearing double wetsuits. We had been told by experienced cruisers that we would find our best snorkeling in the Sea, and Aqua Verde was our favourite spot of the year with the best conditions.

JOANNA'S JOURNAL

We're at Aqua Verde this morning and I went rowing early in the morning then for a swim. Next I had breakfast and am now doing school with Joshua. Mom is rowing and Dad has turned into Dr. Peters! He's tightening everyone's retainers!!

When everybody was ready we went snorkeling a mile away by dinghy. It was the best snorkeling we've ever had since Hawaii! We had lots of fun, then went sailing in the sailing dinghy. We had a great time!

I woke to a colourful sunrise! It proved that the day would be a warm one! Lydia and I got up early; we slipped out and went for a morning sail in the dinghy. There was a nice breeze. After breakfast we went snorkeling which was lots of fun. There many types of fish and underwater canyons that we swam through. It was great! By the way I just learnt Morse Code! Here is the alphabet. (Joanna wrote it out in her journal!) After lunch we went boating. Lydia and I flipped our small dinghy and played in the water with it and with Dad all afternoon! It was fun!

Aqua Verde had a small village within walking distance, and we visited it one morning with our shopping bags and backpacks. We found a very poor, dusty, primitive place with goats, pigs, open wells, stick fences, a little church, gravel playground, neat little school, and a tiny tienda on the porch of a house. I was delighted to find the tienda had a reasonable supply of fresh fruit such as limes, tomatoes, avocados, bananas, vegetables (potatoes), eggs, frozen chicken, oatmeal, and canned goods. It felt like a gold mine to me and we enthusiastically stocked up as much as we could carry. Allan spoke Spanish to the proprietors and we had a pleasant visit with them. It did not seem that they had customers very often and they were chatty and hospitable. To find any supplies on this remote section of the Baja was fortuitous and we were excited with our find. It meant that our journey would be all that much more enjoyable. Fresh food beats canned food any day. As mom and chef, I felt the responsibility of providing interesting and tasty meals for my hungry growing crew.

JOSHUA'S JOURNAL

We had an enjoyable day in Agua Verde when we took the dinghy ashore after breakfast and walked through the small village. We met a boy and his family had forty goats. They draw water from an open well with a pulley like people did one hundred years ago in the early years of America. We found a well-stocked tienda where Mom picked out a few things we needed.

We were led to a small hot springs cove near Point Cosme, by 'Manu Wai' (Cecil and Maria Elena Lange). Cecil was a 75-year-old Kiwi and renowned boat builder who knew every corner of the Sea of Cortez. He wanted to take us to some of the less frequented anchorages in the sea. Hot Springs Cove was a great spot to snorkel and we had a fun afternoon with them hunting for scallops and baking in the hot springs while the tide slowly came in and around the pool to cool us off again.

We had one night anchored in Candeleros Bay which is a small bay protected from south winds. It was a beautiful, quiet spot and we had this lovely little bay all to ourselves. This was the quintessential, ultimate, romantic, idyllic location; words could hardly describe it. We slept well until a north breeze came up sending small waves into the bay. I woke at 04:30, hopped outside into the cockpit to check our water depth. We were sitting in 12 feet of water. It was a little shallow for my comfort zone although we still had five feet of clearance under our keel. We left at 09:30 for Puerto Escondido.

We spent an uneventful day anchored in the 'waiting room,' a small outer bay from Puerto Escondido. We heard from other cruisers that there was no point in going into Puerto Escondido, since it was a large anchorage with very narrow entrance, and not much to do once inside. The remains of a large development lined the bay, with foundations in place, but the developers ran out of money and it was left unfinished. We preferred the wild places, so we continued north for Loreto.

The vessel *Salal* was one day ahead of us and over the radio they were able to recommend good anchorages. It was a great help. The weather was becoming more settled and we experienced only gentle breezes now and calm seas. Air temperature was reaching 90°F during the day, but still cool at night.

The seas were so calm we were able to easily and safely anchor north of the Loreto breakwater and go ashore for three hours. We were low on gasoline for the outboard engine, hence our stop. We also checked in with the Port Captain, something that cruisers are required to do at most posts. We loved the quaint, clean, lovely town centre with its old church, mission, tasteful shops, and historic hotel. We met up with other cruisers for fish tacos at lunchtime in a small local shop. It was by far the best Mexican lunch we had yet. It was so delicious and a real treat. We couldn't stop eating the fish tacos fresh off the grill and we kept ordering more and more.

Loreto was a surprise to us. It had everything there that we needed. It was the most charming small Mexican town we visited. A tree-lined cobblestone lane led from the historical mission to the central plaza. Cafés, galleries and a character hotel added to the atmosphere of this "boutique" Mexican town. We loved it! We found fresh produce, a well-stocked store, a meat store, a place to drop off our garbage, and a public telephone so we could use our pocket e-mailer to contact my folks. Loreto was an enjoyable and efficient stop for us.

The Loreto experience stayed with us—15 years later it became an annual visit and holiday destination. We continue to love that area of the world.

Ballandra Bay on Isla Carmen was beautiful and remote, just nine miles east of Loreto. We arrived at 15:00 and it was hot. This was the first time we experienced really warm swimming water. It was so refreshing to jump into the water and swim. The next day we spent a few hours walking the entire bay. The beachcombing was spectacular and we found a large bank full of fossil shells. It was fascinating to dig into. We found lots of shells as we walked on the shallow rock ledges along the shore. Allan found a green twenty-six-legged brittle starfish. This was something we had not seen before.

At the south point Allan accidentally cornered a baby seagull. The mother, father and all the relatives began to squawk, squeal and dive-bomb Allan and Joshua. It was both amazing and fascinating to see such protective qualities in these birds.

By this point in our cruising we were in the groove of living on the boat and living together. Having perfect conditions and warm weather helped. We were all doing lot of reading, resting, swimming, boating, shell-collecting, and playing board games (Risk, Monopoly, Scrabble were the favourites). The children were becoming more and more enjoyable and cooperative, working better together and with us. I can still see in my mind's eye Joanna and Lydia exploring Ballandra Bay together in our rowboat and enjoying themselves immensely as they sat side-by-side with one oar each.

They thoroughly explored the bay. They loved the freedom.

Next stop was Isla Coronados only 10 miles north of Ballandra Bay. There was a 10 knot northwest wind for perfect sailing conditions. We came through a shallow pass between Coronados and the mainland. Apparently it was the fishing hot spot, so over went the line as we slowly motored through. We caught two fish. Allan and Joshua were ecstatic.

Anchoring on the north side of Coronados Island, a National Park, seemed to work and we were able to get ashore for the afternoon to walk along the sparkling white beach. It was sparkling white to the point of being absolutely dazzling and blinding to the eyes. It was a beach entirely made up of tiny broken shells. Coronado Island is another remarkable spot in the sea different from anywhere else we had been. The white sand beach against the turquoise green water was a beautiful contrast. Inland, it is very barren as it is the remains of a volcano.

There were well-marked trails on the island so we walked a little ways and were struck by the hardiness of the plant life. The landscape was covered with stubby, stocky, dry-looking shrubs with long spindly, sharp, thorny branches. There were buds and tiny colourful flowers on the ends. It was such a hot day we did not feel like walking too far, so we headed back to the boat for a fish dinner.

I sautéed and pan-fried the fish in butter with onions, zucchini, tomato, and lime and my simple mayonnaise sauce served with rice and green beans. Eating couldn't be any better or fresher.

Early the next morning, we picked up our anchor and returned to the fishing spot. In the same place we caught four more yellow-fin tuna. Everyone was thrilled. This was our best fishing yet. We calculated that our fishing license that we were required to buy (costing $500 Canadian) had now resulted in $38 per fish since we had caught a total of 13 fish in Mexican waters.

The next anchorage was the large, wild, and picturesque San Juanico. It has five beautiful beaches lined with striking rock formations and pinnacles throughout the bay. But it was a surprisingly windy spot and we were often changing anchorages to stay out of the wind and rolly swell. Our reward for persevering in this windy place was a couple of great hikes on shore, climbing two small hills to get a fantastic view of the entire area. Allan took some excellent photos. The land of the Baja is tawny, bare, wrinkled, all sand and rocks; it's an arid land of desert.

Our last stop on the Baja Peninsula was Bahia Conception which is a popular destination for Southern Californians. It is beside the Mexican Highway that runs all the way to La Paz and Cabo San Lucas. It can be a very windy place, so we spent a full week safely anchored in front of Santispac. We had the most protection here from the northwest winds of 20 knots that picked up regularly each afternoon. At least it kept things relatively pleasant and cool. The day we visited the town of Mulege for provisions the temperature reached 105ºF (40.6ºC).

JOANNA'S JOURNAL

At Bahia Conception today I woke up with an eagerness to see a new place! The bay here has WARM water! We went clamming and we got tons! We're enjoying it here.

We spent a lot of time in the really warm water in Conception Bay. The children lived in their swim suits and were in and out of the water continuously. The resident sea turtle kept us busy, causing us to look over the side whenever we heard deep breathing coming from somewhere beside us. The clamming was fantastic. In half an hour we had a pail full of steamers that we collected by diving in a few feet of water at Pelican Reef. Joshua spent an afternoon fishing for bottom fish off our boat. In two hours he caught seven fish. They were delicious, the meat resembling our trout, making a perfect meal for our family of five. The beach combing here was excellent and we found murexes, olives, colourful scallop shells, and the tiny translucent jingles that Lydia made into a mobile.

LYDIA'S JOURNAL

Today we had a very long swim. Joshua went fishing and caught 7 small cat fish. They look like small sharks.

JOSHUA'S JOURNAL

Our week in Conception Bay has been great! We are surrounded by lots of friends on their boats. One day we went for a five mile hike with some other cruisers. There were a lot of lizards hiding, which I attempted to catch. I did not catch any. We played volleyball games on the beach. I have done some fishing! And it is getting really really HOT here!

The weather continued to get hotter and hotter. It did not cool down at night anymore, and even with all of our fans going all night we were starting to get more and more uncomfortable. Baja is a land of extreme winds and temperatures. I felt it was time to cross the Sea to San Carlos after spending one and a half weeks in Conception Bay. Allan agreed.

Our trip across the Sea ended after an uneventful 90-mile night sail to San Carlos. In Mexico we were getting quite used to flaming red sunsets, clear starry skies, sunny hot days, the rising full moon that sent a highway of light across the water, pods of leaping porpoises, the occasional whale, and the ubiquitous pelican making spectacular dives for his dinner every few seconds. As we approached San Carlos the two jagged peaks that clearly mark the harbour and anchorage stood out against the horizon.

San Carlos is one of two hurricane holes in Mexico, the other being Puerto Vallarta. We chose San Carlos because it has a huge parking lot area for boats to be on land. It is well out of the hurricane zone, and we felt comfortable leaving the boat there for the winter. The haul-out was straightforward and well organized. We were confident our boat would be secure and safe for the winter months which was an important consideration because it represented a huge financial investment to us. We could leave *Morning*, our floating home for the past year, until next spring when we could make plans to get the boat back to Vancouver.

When, staunchly entering port, after long ventures, hauling up, worn and old, batter'd by sea and wind, torn by many a fight, with original sailing on all gone, replaced or mended, I only saw at last, the beauty of the ship...
—*Walt Whitman*

CHAPTER 33
Haul-Out

Anchored in the San Carlos harbour was pleasant for a few nights until a lot of swell came in and we were rolling and bouncing a lot. It became difficult to work on the boat in these conditions but by then we were able to get a slip in the full marina.

It was also getting a lot hotter. We were fortunate to have access to a swimming pool and that became a part of our afternoon routine. There was a lot of work that needed to be done on the boat in preparation for haul-out. In such heat, it was challenging to feel like doing anything. Sleeping at night was becoming more and more difficult.

Haul out happened on Friday, June 2 and *Morning* was moved to dry storage. Ed Grossman was the owner of the large facility and was the tractor man who towed us to the parking lot. We were all allowed to stay in the cockpit of the boat throughout the haul-out and the tow to the storage lot. It was terrific fun and felt like we were sailing on the highway through the desert! The children loved it because it was kind of a weird experience, driving along on land sitting in the cockpit of your offshore sailboat. Not exactly what *Morning* was designed for.

We were impressed with Mr. Grossman's steering and were thankful to be hauled out at high tide more or less on time with our assigned schedule. Once on shore we were two storeys off the ground, high above the car traffic. It was quite a view from that perspective. Everything went smoothly. The dry storage area was spacious and Allan was pleased with the setup. Ironically we were parked right next to *Neener 3*, the boat Joshua had saved from destruction in the manta ray rescue. It is a very small world in the boating community.

JOANNA'S JOURNAL

Beautiful San Carlos! It is so so hot out!

When it was time to haul out the boat at 1:00 pm I was excited! We motored over to the ramp and were met by a big travel trailer with remote controls. The trailer slided under us. We were in the cockpit all the time! When the boat is out of the water the cockpit was 2 storeys up and we were travelling at a pretty fast rate up in the air! It was a very weird feeling to be travelling on a road on a boat! We were at the yard at last and the boat got set up. We climbed down then headed for the pool.

There was one week to prepare *Morning*, removing her from the water and getting her on land for her winter in dusty, dry San Carlos before we had arranged to leave for home. Allan and Joshua worked incredibly hard, sanding the entire hull, plugging the through-hulls, cleaning and polishing the propeller, checking the zincs, covering the boat, and removing all the lines. Joanna and Lydia stayed with me and together we made meals, did the shopping, packed up our gear, completed school work, and updated journals. Every day we walked to the storage yard to take Allan and Joshua their lunch. Joshua was an amazing helper for his dad. They did so much work in the extreme heat. It was remarkable, at the same time, to watch the Mexican men play soccer in the parking lot at lunch time in their long pants and jeans in such heat.

JOSHUA'S JOURNAL

One of the main jobs that Dad and I did was wet-sand the bottom of our hull, an ordeal which took seven hours. We were exhausted at the end of it, but our boat was ready to be left for the winter.

We moved off the boat into a small local Mexican motel the day it became really unbearably hot at night. To be in an air conditioned hotel meant we could all sleep well and then feel like working during the day. Taking the boat out of the water and storing her for the winter season involved a great deal of organization on Allan's part, so to have a 'get-away' off from the boat at this time was helpful. There was a full bathroom with shower—a luxury for us boaters—a small kitchenette completely stocked with dishes, full fridge, hot plate so I could "camp-out" and still make hot meals, and enough beds for us all to sleep on. The air conditioner was the main feature and made the last week in San Carlos tolerable.

LYDIA'S JOURNAL

At the haul out ramp, the truck came and positioned the rig underneath our boat. They slowly raised us out of the water and the tractor pushed us down the highway. We were sitting in the cockpit at the time! It was a very weird feeling being moved along the deserts of Mexico when we are supposed to be in the water! We were so high up. When we got to the storage yard they put us up on stands and left us.

I have noticed that most men when they enter a barber shop and must wait their turn, drop into a chair and pick up a magazine. I simply sit down and pick up the thread of my sea wanderings, which began more than fifty years ago and is not quite ended. There is hardly a waiting room in the east that has not served as my cockpit, whether I was waiting to board a train or to see a dentist. And I am usually still trimming sheets when the train starts or drill begins to whine.

—E.B. White

CHAPTER 34

Home

LYDIA'S JOURNAL

June 9: We are leaving for Tuscan today!! In the morning Dad and Joshua got the last few things from the boat. We packed up all the bags and at 9 am we left on a local bus to Guaymas where the main bus station is. It was quite a hassle to get the ten big heavy bags to the bus station. We had tickets for our bus at 11 am. We waited til it came. It is a large first class bus with comfortable seats, TV, air conditioning, bathroom and curtains. We started on our way. It was very barren desert countryside with a few bushes and plants and trees and sometimes a large cactus.

Our trip home was getting closer and closer. I couldn't believe we had actually been away for an entire year with our family living on *Morning*. We had seen and experienced so much. It seemed strange that the grand adventure had suddenly come to an end. We had lived the dream. And even though Allan had been hopeful to circumnavigate, I knew that we had accomplished what we needed to. The year had its challenges and rewards, but overall it had been a year of tremendously hard work on the part of Allan and myself.

I sensed the children were ready to go home. In fact, without saying anything, I knew they wanted to go home.

The trip with all the preparation and sacrifice involved, had been no holiday, but it was an experience of a lifetime, a legacy that we gave our children to make a difference in their lives.

Travelling on the bus through Mexico north to the border and then to Tucson was a major transition for all of us. It was time to consider and process what we had experienced.

Entering into the United States was a sudden reverse culture shock.

My first impressions formed as words and phrases came to my mind: English spoken, four lane highways, traffic, busy, processed, strip malls, fast food, sterile, concrete, crowds of people, "hurry up," no time to talk, no eye contact or smiles.

Allan found a modest motel for us to stay in for a few days before our plane flight left for Vancouver. Even though it was the most basic motel, it had housekeeping service every day, fresh towels and large comfortable beds. Within walking distance along a very busy road, there were fast food restaurants, but no fresh grocery outlets. Our stomachs had to make a major readjustment after the natural fresh food we had enjoyed for seven months in Mexico.

JOSHUA'S JOURNAL

Our bags are ready and packed in the car for the plane flight tomorrow. I am very every excited about going home!! On the air plane I got a window seat so the view was awesome. There was a lot of desert until we got closer to Denver, Colorado when it got greener and snow appeared. I thank the Lord for giving our family the opportunity to experience what we did on the sailboat!!

The day of our flight home arrived, and we headed for the airport. We noticed the contrast in the type of people we saw. Well-dressed professionals filled the terminal. We missed the hustle bustle and noise of the passionate Mexican people chattering in Spanish.

Before we knew it we got off the airplane in Vancouver. How simple and fast it was to get home compared to the huge effort and time (months) it took to get to Mexico! The renters in our house had moved out so we were able to move back into our home and set up again. Our furniture had been packed into the garage. The children enthusiastically set up their rooms and personal things.

For the next two weeks I was in a daze. The adjustment took some time for me. For one thing I felt the same boat motion as though I was still on the boat. When the motion settled down a few weeks later, I had the house put back together and we were back into routines. The children checked in with friends and we started to plan our summer.

Allan and I had the difficult discussion about whether to continue our travels on the boat. He agreed that it was best thing to stop while everything was a positive memory.

The Mazatlan experience when we rolled gunnel to gunnel in a helpless condition had caused him to seriously reconsider thoughts of circumnavigation. As if to confirm our change of plans, Allan had two projects waiting for him to begin when we returned home. I had sent newsletters to all of our clients (four times during the year) as well as updates to our local newspaper. I did not realize how many people were vicariously travelling with us.

When we put on a slideshow for our community, for example, we had a full house. People we did not even know filled a local community hall, enthusiastic to hear our stories and watch our slide show. We put on a total of 35 presentations as a family to both small and large groups. The largest presentation was at the Bluewater Cruising Association meeting for a few hundred people. Our children did much of the speaking, Joshua played the piano, Joanna played her flute, and it was a lot of fun to share our dream and our story.

I do not want to minimize the transition we all experienced on our return home. Allan and I had the least amount of difficulty re-entering our Canadian culture. But for our children it was more of a challenge. This caught us unawares, since they had no trouble leaving home at all. But to re-enter Canadian culture and to return to school was not as easy.

In retrospect, there are many considerations for a family to make when they consider a major trip like the one we did as well as years of preparation.

Are we glad we did it? Absolutely. It changed our lives and caused us to deeply appreciate our home, our country, our family, each other.

Do we recommend other families do it? Absolutely. You can leave a legacy of memory with your children. It is the greatest gift you can give them.

He picked up the ball of twine and put it to his nose and drew in a smell of boats-caulking smell, rope locker smell- the smell which, savored in the deepest gloom of wintertime, had the power of evoking faraway wave tops, a canted mast, splashing bow-waves, a warm summer breeze on a helmsman's cheek.

—*John Hershey*

CHAPTER 35

Twenty Years Later

The Amigo Net is still going strong.

After our family was launched, Allan and I bought *Morning II*, a 36-foot Bavaria sailboat, to replace our beloved *Morning*. As a couple, we wanted to relive the dream, but in the local inland waters of the Pacific Northwest and Desolation Sound.

To backtrack 20 years, once we arrived home to Bowen Island we had the winter to figure out how to get *Morning* back after exploring many alternatives. *Morning* was sailed back home via Hawaii by friends of ours, Neil and Esther Symons and crew. When *Morning* returned, we kept her for one more year. The highlight was spending a two-month summer on *Morning* enjoying familiar sailing grounds at the north end of Georgia Strait, beyond to Desolation Sound and the Broughton Archipelago. We loved our family time together, but came to the conclusion that owning an offshore sailboat was a huge investment and it was time to sell her. Surprisingly we sold her in a matter of days. We purchased a small cruising motor boat, a 26-foot Commander that Allan used for a number of years primarily for his work, travelling to remote house building sites around Howe Sound.

Our children completed high school and went on to obtain university degrees. Joshua graduated in Political Science and History, Joanna in Fine Arts, and Lydia in Biology.

Our children are very active young people and we have been amazed with their dedication to having their own adventures, keeping fit, and pursuing extreme sports. They are exceptionally well rounded individuals with a passion for life and living. They all went on to complete post graduate training; Joshua in communications, Joanna as an RMT (registered massage therapist) and Lydia as a doctor.

For myself, I gained a new appreciation for the world beyond our borders and the amazing adventures we can experience if we are willing to take the risk. It was a remarkable bonding time that we had with our family. Faith sustained me.

Allan has continued with his successful design and construction business. The one year off to sail was a marvellous change of scene for Allan. It gave him new energy, motivation and inspiration for his work. It has given him great pleasure to look back over the years to what it means to follow the dream. He is overwhelmingly grateful for the opportunity and experience we had to own and sail *Morning* for a year offshore, with our family.

Boating again in local waters is a wonderful experience for Allan and me to enjoy together. We travel at a slow pace, enjoying all the delightful anchorages and marinas in the Pacific Northwest. In our opinion, these are the best cruising grounds in the world. We love to go out for weeks at a time, reliving our boat travel itineraries from 20 years ago. We have rediscovered our favourite anchorages. We enjoy the camaraderie of the local boating community. We are thankful to have the health and resources to be able to do what we love.

We hope this little volume will encourage others to pursue "the dream."

From our adult children

My parents gave me the gift of expanding my horizons beyond life of growing up on a small island on the BC West Coast. I learned to respect the power of the seas—and the importance of faith! It was a unique and special experience and a highlight of my life I will forever hold dear in my heart!
—Joshua

Three things I learned from the trip, I have since put into practice in my life. I learned to never establish ideas about a place before getting there. I learned to be comfortable being uncomfortable. I learned to never romanticize an idea (like sailing offshore), but instead I get excited while staying realistic about a new (hard) challenge.
—Joanna

Being given the opportunity to escape "normal life" for a year and explore, learn, innovate and create is something that has inspired me well into adulthood. It has shaped, in many ways, how I view life to be lived; one of interest, challenge and awe of the natural world. I look fondly back on this childhood experience and the gift my parents gave us.
—Lydia

CPSIA information can be obtained
at www.ICGtesting.com
Printed in the USA
BVHW060002121221
623700BV00004B/5